Beyond the Walls: The Rise of Digital Information and its Impact on Cultural Heritage

Chandrika

Table of Contents

Chapter 1: Introduction 1

1.1 Introduction 1

1.2 Research background 3

1.3 Research question 4

1.4 Research problem 5

1.5 Objectives of the study 5

1.6 Rationale 6

1.7 Definitions of related terms 7

1.8 Research methodology 8

1.8.1 Research design 8

1.9 Limitations 9

1.10. Chapter outline 9

1.11 Annexures outline 10

Chapter 2: Literature Review 11

2.1 Introduction 11

2.2 Theoretical framework 11

2.3 Museum objects 13

2.3.1 Museum curatorship 14

2.4 Digital technology in a museum 15

2.4.1 Digital curatorship 17

2.5 Digitisation and digital preservation 18

2.6 Classification of cultural objects 20

2.6.1 Classification and taxonomies 21

2.6.2 Representation of cultural objects in a museum 2.7 Colonisation and museum objects of curiosity **Chapter 3: Methodology** 24

26

28

3.1 Introduction 28

3.2 Research approach 28

3.3 Ethical considerations 29

3.4 Data collection 30

3.4.1 A case study 30

3.4.2 Online questionnaire 31

3.4.3 Purposive sampling 32

3.4.4 Summary of population and sample size 33

3.4.5 Document analysis 33

3.4.6 Exhibition review 34

3.5 Data validity and reliability 35

3.6 Summary 36

Chapter 4: Data Analysis and Presentation of Findings 37

4.1 Introduction 37

4.2 Data analysis approach 37

4.2.1 Content analysis 37

4.2.2 Iziko Museums' online presence 38

4.2.3 Archive-based records 39

4.2.4 Exhibition review 43

4.3 Data presentation 47

4.3.1 Description of data collection 48

4.3.2 Data analysis of questions about core functions in the museum 48

4.3.3 Data analysis of questions about art collections management 50

4.3.4 Data analysis of digital preservation questions 53

4.4 Summary 58

Chapter 5: Findings, Discussion, Recommendations and Suggestions for Future Research 60

5.1 Introduction 60

5.2 Findings 60

5.3 Discussions 61

5.3.1 Decolonising museum objects 61

5.3.2 Museum ethics 62

5.4 Recommendations 63

5.5 Suggestions for future research 64

5.6 Closing remarks 64

Reference List   67

Appendices   76

Appendix A: Informed Consent   76

Appendix B: Email Invitation for an Online Questionnaire   77

Appendix C: Online Questions from the REDCap Hyperlink   78

Appendix D: Permission to Conduct Research from Iziko   81

Appendix E: Iziko Digitization Policy of 2014-10-21   82

Appendix F: ISANG Art Acquisitions Committee Terms of Reference   91

Appendix G: Iziko 2003 - 2004 Annual Report   95

Appendix H: Hidden Treasures Exhibition Photographs   97

Appendix I: Mr. Max Leipold Masks Bequest   100

Chapter 1: Introduction

1.1 Introduction

The increasing demand for instant access to, and dissemination of, digital information is likely to change the way knowledge related to physical cultural objects is produced and managed. This is especially true for cultural institutions and their associated practices, which are constantly transforming in response to broader societal and technical developments. For instance, as cultural institutions actively convert more of their documents and data to digital formats, they are affected by the pace and intensity at which information is growing, which means that they have to shift to online platforms by reorienting, integrating and developing elaborate ways of mediating their collections both inside and outside their institutionally defined boundaries.

Although museums are adept at dealing with the representation of cultural objects, they are constantly devising new ways of representing different cultural objects curatorially. Part of this involves providing authoritative content in an environment where competing narratives and interpretations exist. In the past two decades, digital technologies have become ubiquitous in museums. Digital technology has changed the way that museums document, collect, research, curate, preserve and display information, as well as how they make that information accessible to visitors (Chowdhury & Ruthven, 2015:11).

Since cultural institutions are investing in emerging digital technologies, such as electronic devices, data management systems and cataloguing, many museums are evolving curatorially by embracing digital technologies as a tool for engaging the public and for disseminating information about the museum collections. However, in the case of curatorial mediation, the importance of properly representing digitised cultural heritage objects cannot be overemphasised. This means that museum practitioners should actively think about understanding both the cultural history and current context of the object. For instance, in the South African context some digital heritage preservation methods reflect the "battle around how the sediments of colonial and post-apartheid history are being used, collected and interpreted" (Autry, 2017:120). This debate is important because the introduction of digital culture into museums means that present-day curators face new challenges regarding representation.

The classification of creators of cultural objects as "unknown" potentially deprives object makers of any substantial acknowledgment, especially when a significant number of object makers are assigned anomalous curatorial values (Stocking, 1985:237). It is even more problematic when cultural objects are assigned lower aesthetic value without any concerted effort to conduct in-depth research about who created the objects and what they represent. This is important because members of the public have to interpret the limited information available to them in order to understand the value of the object or to seek an authoritative explanation of the object maker's provenance (Van Beurden, 2015:150).

This challenge is exacerbated by the public's expectation that museums are able to balance the demand to observe, acknowledge, and even celebrate differences. However, the "unknown" status of some creators perpetuates a culture of objectification in the museum discourse, because many objects in public collections, as well as their associated museum practices, bear remnants of the colonial past. In South Africa, for example, the collapse of apartheid and its associated ways of defining identity, history, and culture resulted in an urgent push to recast the past and attempt to assemble histories that included the voices of people who had been written out of the national story (Autry, 2017:120).

In the past, museums were widely recognised as places of specialised knowledge and enlightenment, and much of what is displayed in a museum is trusted to be authentic. Poster (2001:21-23) points out that the real object that is "encased and enclosed by the museum is rendered authentic or privileged by the associated apparatuses of scholarship and institutional authority which is different from a manipulated digital object that is materially unstable in a way that the real object is not." A digital object composed of bytes and digits can easily be re-formatted, re-aligned, re-coloured, cropped, erased or altered. Essentially, the museum context confers authoritative authenticity on both written and visual texts, and other objects. This status of "authenticity is recursively affirmed by the public's expectation of experiencing real things in public museums" (Davison, 1991:97).

However, authenticity is not only present in the object but is also projected onto its community of origin and proceeds from "assumptions about temporality, wholeness, and continuity" (Van Beurden, 2015:52).

In summary, when museum objects find expression as distinct objects, or digits used to represent something in the real-world, digital curatorship will inevitably be required to maintain an intimate relationship between the real and the virtual world. Moreover, defining curatorial standards and processes for collating descriptive data as historical evidence will become even more urgent. Equally, within the museum discourse, the word "unknown" in the term "unknown maker" functions as a deficient link or inference that impedes digital curatorship, and only intensifies the challenge of creating a balance between the preservation of knowledge and the accurate representation of cultural material.

1.2 Research background

The South African Department of Arts and Culture acknowledges that the digital revolution is fundamentally altering how cultural goods and services are produced, distributed, marketed and accessed. In the spirit of disseminating and sharing knowledge, the Department of Arts and Culture's *National Third White Paper on The Digitisation of Heritage Resources* (2010:21) highlights the need for universal access to digital heritage, where digitisation is seen as an enabler of the right of access to information as stipulated in section 32 of the Constitution of the Republic of South Africa. Therefore, the Department is encouraging cultural institutions to put mechanisms in place to create and manage digitisation programmes.

It is necessary to locate the use of digitisation firmly within the context of public art collections, specifically for recording and documenting heritage material that will allow public cultural institutions to preserve and share information about South Africa's heritage. To this end, all custodians of heritage material that operate under the Department of Arts and Culture are required to develop a digitisation strategy that aligns with the White Paper, taking into consideration the recommendations by the South African Heritage Resource

Agency. The "digitisation strategy for each custodian should reflect the unique characteristics of the institution including: its legislative mandate; its identified stakeholders and beneficiaries; the nature of the collections being managed, and institution-specific collection management processes and policies" (Department of Arts and Culture, 2010:42-43).

Considering the current local struggles, including the legacy of apartheid and the shortcomings of various cultural public institutions in relation to digital custodianship, a new digital generation is nonetheless emerging. Since the end of apartheid, there has been a need to actively address existing inaccuracies about the past through digital decolonisation projects in an attempt to rewrite the lived experiences of indigenous and marginalised groups.

The current local decolonisation discourse, which continues to rage on various public platforms, serves as a compelling reason to engage with the digital profiling of "unknown maker(s)", particularly when there are traces of liberal academic curiosity in studying cultural objects from the mid-20th century to the 1990s. Under the South African autocratic apartheid government, the pervasive effects of racial segregation and the range of policies that deliberately aimed to reinforce cultural differences were evident in the obscure classification practices of the time, in which certain cultural group experiences and artistic traditions were systematically ignored, misrepresented or marginalised in mainstream museums (Autry, 2017:99).

1.3 Research question

The main research question was: "Is there a curatorial framework(s) that is used, or can be used, to digitally profile "unknown maker(s)" of cultural objects adequately?"

To assist with answering the main research question, this study asked two sub-questions:

- What content or descriptive metadata is being used for the classification of "unknown maker(s)" in the digitisation of national art collections?

- What reasonable precautions can a museum take to ensure that the digital classification of "unknown" identities does not perpetuate ethically unsound narratives when transferring them from the physical collection into the digital space?

1.4 Research problem

The museification of cultural institutions is one method of preserving the past, but it implies that without it, indigenous communities would fade into obscurity, although they are problematically portrayed as other, exotic, unchanging and disconnected from the present (Morphy, 1999:20).

In the context of a national museum, this study focussed on the process of digitising public art collections, and cast light on some of the ethical problems that could possibly emerge in relation to the current digital preservation framework(s), particularly those applied to cultural objects, including the use of tools for ingesting data, and managing, accessing and reusing digital objects from ISANG's official records.

Museums are still plagued by colonial museological systems even though they are moving towards decentralising and democratising their collections. In this regard, the digital augmentation of ahistorical information, restitution, and decolonialisation of museums foregrounds a need to redress the historical injustice museums might have caused by revising the inherent cataloguing and classification methods. This is crucial to restoring the agency of "unknown maker(s)" of cultural objects as producers of their intellectual and aesthetic history within contemporary museum work.

1.5 Objectives of the study

This study was designed to investigate current digital curation practices regarding cultural objects catalogued with an "unknown maker(s)" classificatory label. This research explored the practical and technical challenges that arose when dealing with the digital profiling of "unknown maker(s)" in public art collections, by examining how the Iziko South African

National Gallery (ISANG) museum currently catalogues and presents objects created by "unknown maker(s)".

1.6 Rationale

The digital profiling of "unknown maker(s)" of cultural objects necessitates an ongoing investigation into issues of language, identity, authorship, semiotic weight, cultural heritage and the supposed democratisation involved in access to, and future usage of, digital cultural heritage objects. Failing to address the potential indignity of representing the maker of a cultural object as "unknown" may exacerbate inequalities by perpetuating them in a digital curation system. The correlation between culture and language is embedded in cultural objects, enabling us to identify and deduce information about them. Thus, inaccurate data can produce inconsistent information, which can pose a serious threat to good digital curatorial practice. If digital curatorship and preservation activities are not undertaken, or are neglected, the ability of the institution to successfully take care of the digital objects, and accompanying information, will be negatively affected (Wanless, 2007:16).

Whatever the controversy over the use of the word "unknown" in the term "unknown maker", cultural institutions can no longer afford to passively digitise or profile "unknown maker(s)" of cultural objects based solely on a lack of clear classification terms. As for the term "unknown maker", it is hoped that the terminology or definition adopted in this study will avoid the problems associated with using such a vague term particularly in relation to the reproduction of unconscionable narratives because of insufficient or unavailable information. This is important because knowing about the object's origins can result in emotional and intellectual responses from which judgements, based on those responses, can be made (Davison, 1991:141).

1.7 Definitions of related terms

Authenticity refers to an original work of art as having to exist in a unique space and time. Walter Benjamin (1936:143-144) defines authenticity as

> [an] aura that can be possessed only by an original work of art but the reproduction of works of art in modern times causes the loss of the aura and the loss of authenticity in the aesthetic experience. The aura distinguishes the viewer from the work and creates the necessary detachment for a true aesthetic experience.

Cultural objects refers to a "collection of objects, or a type of object adapted by human workmanship with historical significance, or objects to which oral traditions are attached and which are associated with living heritage, objects of scientific or technological interest" (SAHRA, 1999:S,32e-h). Examples of cultural objects can be found in disciplines such as architecture, sculpture, painting, music, photography, textiles and digital media.

Digital curation is the management and preservation of digital material to ensure accessibility over the long-term. Digital curation also includes maintaining and adding value to a trusted body of digital information for future and current use; specifically, the active management and appraisal of data over the entire life cycle (Abbott, 2008).

Digital collection refers to "the body of acquired objects held in title by museums and all objects in digital form in the museum collection, whether born-digital or digitised" (International Standard ISO/DIS 18461:2016).

Cultural institution is a term used to define "institutions with an acknowledged mission to engage in the conservation, interpretation, and dissemination of cultural, scientific, and environmental knowledge, and promote activities meant to inform and educate citizens on associated aspects of culture, history, science, and the environment" (Borowiecki, Forbes & Fresa, 2006:300). Examples of cultural institutions include libraries, museums, historical sites and community art centres.

The term **"unknown maker(s)"** will be used in this study to refer to unidentified makers/creators of cultural objects which are designated or classified as indistinct, strange or exotic (Henning, 2005:22).

1.8 Research methodology

Data triangulation was used because it is "a research strategy that cuts across the qualitative-quantitative divide which is consistent with a pluralist theoretical viewpoint" (Olsen, 2004:23). There should not be "a contradiction between the interaction of quantitative and qualitative modes of research, rather it should be possible to bring them together to shed light on any chosen social research topic" (Olsen, 2004:3).

This study utilised data triangulation, a multi-method strategy that allows the researcher to use a variety of "data sources, such as archival records, physical objects, direct observation, surveys and literature reviews to collect data" (Yin, 2009:102). Data triangulation is recommended for this type of research because of its multi-perspective meta-interpretations. The study also used a single case study approach, which focussed on ISANG, and collected data from the Iziko institutions by using an online questionnaire, museum archival records, content analysis, and an exhibition review.

Objects that were listed in the ISANG art collections as having "unknown maker(s)" were selected for this project. The research made use of purposive sampling, inviting responses from the body of Iziko's museum professionals who were invited to participate in an online questionnaire. The REDCap Software web tool was used for the descriptive analysis of the data that was collected.

1.8.1 Research design

The research was supported by a case study that drew attention to the problems that digital classification presents in the museum environment. The case study provided useful data, some of which came from Iziko's published catalogues. These catalogues provided information regarding the selected objects and how they were curated.

1.9 Limitations

ISANG, located in Cape Town, was the only institution to which the researcher was able to gain access. Therefore, the study was only able to access a limited number of cultural objects associated with "unknown maker(s)". Furthermore, the short period of time in which this research was conducted restricted the scope of the study. There was also a limited amount of primary research material available, such as exhibition reviews, journals and museum publications on cultural objects, or prior research available on the digital classification of "unknown maker(s)" of cultural objects, that focussed on South African art museums.

1.10 Chapter outline

The first chapter introduces the research topic and explains the rationale behind the study.

The second chapter reviews existing and relevant literature from other researchers, and provides a theoretical background for the research topic. This chapter also organises theoretical views, indicating how previous research informs this study.

The third chapter describes the research design. It provides a comprehensive description of the methods and procedures used to collect data, including ethical considerations and the data analysis process.

The fourth chapter presents the findings of the study based on the analysis of the collected data and the theory used to inform the study.

The fifth chapter concludes this study with a summary of the research findings and makes recommendations for future research.

1.11 Annexures outline

Documentary materials held in a museum constitute a vast resource. However, this study also included official published annexures from Iziko including documents such as the 2004 digitisation policy, extracts from the 2003/4 Iziko annual report, inventory and catalogue cards as well as photographs from the 2017 *Hidden Treasures* exhibition. This selected auxiliary documentation and the usage of its contents provided substantial data in support of the triangulation research methodology utilised, where a multi-method strategy approach was applied.

Chapter 2: Literature Review

2.1 Introduction

This literature review has been divided into interrelated themes, and discusses theories concerned with representation and the preservation of museum collections. It explores the literature available on digital curatorship and examines different theoretical frameworks used in museum curatorship practices. It also provides an overview of the current usage status of the term "unknown maker" within the museum context, by focussing on the important contributions made by the Iziko Museums of South Africa towards decolonising museum information.

2.2 Theoretical framework

In his publication *Icon and Images* (1974), Denis Williams claims that a relationship exists between anthropologists, aesthetes, scholars of form and semioticians that feeds imputation and misunderstanding, as reports undertaken by European scholars on Africa show an absence of seriousness on their part. The decision by European scholars to study indigenous cultures as an enforced study deliberately omitted the lived experiences of the formerly oppressed colonised communities and was motivated by the necessity to legitimise colonial administrative and political power (Williams, 1974:29-30).

Inspired by the social sciences, many noteworthy postcolonial scholars have been interrogating the notion or concept of "being" by offering different perspectives on the critique of scientific knowledge. Cristopher Alexander Udofia (2016:10-12) offers the contentious theoretical position that, while Europeans proposed "a conception of being, Africans conceive of force, where Europeans see concrete beings, Africans see concrete forces, a notion that stems not from what they know but rather from what they do not know." Although critical in the recognition of the known and unknown, most differences in rigid classificatory schema do not necessarily have historical validity or accord with the self-identity of people so defined.

In his ontological framework, Udofia (2016:2-3) uses the notion of "force" to illustrate that "African people do not engage themselves in anything that does not serve a specific purpose because utility or function is a fundamental dimension of African social life", which constitutes a plural paradigm of knowing. However, it must also be noted that "force" is not for Africans, a necessary, irreducible attribute of being.

By using a range of pertinent postcolonial theories, and reflecting on the complexities of cultural classification schema and their relevance in contemporary museum collections, this study critically assessed the use of the term "unknown maker", and considered how to improve the way in which creators of cultural objects are recorded in order to appropriately represent their identities.

Against this theoretical backdrop many questions have been raised regarding the ontological schema used to describe cultural objects. Many scholars connect the question of ontology to history and the study of cultural norms because pre-colonial cultural objects, untainted by the influence of Western modernism, are assumed to be prime carriers of culture. However, a serious engagement with a range and depth of cultural objects has led to disagreements about how to name and account for fundamental lived ontologies, because labels such as "unknown" identities or provenance of cultural objects have unintended repercussions associated with their material representation (Kelly, 2014:1). Within museum discourse, the word "unknown" seems to suggest that it is possible to nullify or denounce an identity.

As far as the adopted theoretical framework is concerned, this study argues against the hypothesis that the status of an artefact is always in flux, that is to say that although most museum objects become a work of art separate from their creator, their original meaning should be retained. When cultural objects are taken away from their owners and placed in collections or recontextualised they acquire a new meaning, which is not always related to their original use or purpose.

It is, however, safe to conclude that an outsider who is hampered by a "lack of both the language and culture of a particular community distorted by a translator untrained in the techniques of preserving or gathering information will find it difficult, if not impossible to get to the fundamentals of other people's cultures" (Okon, 2013:99).

2.3 Museum objects

Although museum objects are a subject of research and a source of intellectual stimuli through a mediated experience, some academics see museum objects as a social construct that could help society explain a universal story of human history. Museums are preoccupied with the things that surround us and the politics of representation. French historian Pierra Nora (1996:200-225) suggests that museums are memory machines, a "technical means by which societies remember and organise the past for the purposes of the present. They are a product of societies, which have a historical consciousness by treating material things as evidence or documents of past events."

In the late nineteenth century, museums were created as an important means to understanding the world. They are like laboratories where theoretical concepts in cultural material can be applied in practice and provide a means of acquainting many visitors with such concepts (Guiart, 1983:135-6). According to Jean Guiart (1983:135), museums inherit their roots from the world of the past, seeking to collect evidence of man's cultural heritage in different social settings. This has, however, presented a number of challenges for museums, which ought to be looked at afresh, especially when showcasing cultural objects that are historically and symbolically associated with *Wunderkammern* or cabinets of curiosities.

Kirshenblatt-Gimblett (2004:58) states that "authenticity, uniqueness, and originality constitute the foundation of today's museum collections, where artefacts or objects of curiosity become museum objects by virtue of being redefined, segmented, detached" and recontextualised by curators and researchers. Broadly defined, "the mission of museums is to maintain the intelligibility of objects, which are meaningful and valuable objects. Despite the apparent simplicity of this goal, its attainment is highly problematic" (Domínguez, 2014:617) because cultural objects often become representative of unjustified concepts. There is a practice of objectification in the way that museum cultural objects have been conscripted into the same narrative (Guiart, 1983:136).

Against this backdrop, "many museum institutions were products of an outsider's curiosity, seeking the primitive elements, the exotica, rather than the cultural differences, which made up the rich mosaic of indigenous civilization" (Guiart, 1983:135-6). Museums traditionally prioritise objects and tend towards permanence and the unique, rather than ephemeral reproductions. Although museums claim "to maintain the dimension of the object's original function, it is no more than a claim because the object has been irreparably cut off from this function" (Henning, 2005:1865). Mauss (1969:245) asserts that "the misunderstandings between the African and European cultures are based purely on a blind obeisance to colonial usage and written in an underserved and fortuitous way because of the role played by fetishism."

From the perspective of museums, curatorial problems related to the interpretation and attribution of meaning to cultural objects have passed through several phases that reflect changes in society. The avant-garde museums of the early twentieth century rejected the preservation of what was perceived as the "dead past" in favour of new technologies associated with speed and immediacy that had greater relevance to the present. Yet these new technologies themselves would extend the "realm of the dead" into the present through digital recordings and archiving (Henning, 2005:74).

2.3.1 Museum curatorship

Museum curatorship has recently received much attention because the curator occupies the role of an expert who delivers knowledge or educational information about a collection's objects to an audience. A more contemporary concept of a curator is that of a collaborator, facilitator, arranger, interpreter, storyteller or a moderator of conversations about the objects in an exhibit (Proctor, 2010:38). As the impact of technological advancement increases, digital curatorship has influenced the preservation and dissemination of cultural objects, and new technologies are being used to preserve a "rapidly disappearing material culture, together with the human knowledge and skills that have created it" (Parry, 2007:166).

New technology is characterised by its ability to separate objects, scenes and people from their fixed place in space and time, and "allows them or their forensic traces to circulate as multiple reproductions that threaten the aura of the unique object by making it available for close inspection by a mass audience" (Brown, 2001:16).

Kress (2010) concedes that appreciation for new modes of communication and, sometimes, cultural similarities, inspire museum practitioners to engage in the production of knowledge in previously unimagined ways. This has enabled a detailed account of how new technologies interact with both social and cultural materials.

2.4 Digital technology in a museum

There is no doubt that postcolonial thinking in contemporary museums faces difficulties with finding meaning in symbols, objects and signs, be they analogue, digital or virtual reality. Broadly speaking, with the realisation that information is critical to preserving history, cultural institutions need to consistently curate and store information seamlessly. Initially, one may visualise cultural institutions like libraries, museums, theatres and galleries in their physical form. However, cultural institutions are quickly realising that they need to build their online presence to provide their patrons with access to their ever-growing information (Chowdhury & Ruthven, 2015:9).

Therefore, museum curatorship requires the ability to work productively with digital knowledge and participate in digital networks of collaboration and co-creation (Andrews et al., 2012). As Domínguez (2014) has noted, museum curatorship needs to be understood in complex relation to driving innovation and spearheading digital adoption, while taking into consideration the impact that socio-technical change is having on long-established institutional norms.

With the rapid development of digital technology in the twenty-first century, many museum practitioners are adopting modern strategies and innovative approaches to showcasing their rare collections. As such, modern museum curatorship has grown into a well-observed sector, trusted by many stakeholders to store and preserve tangible and intangible resources that will be available for many generations to come.

As digital technology finds its expression in museums, digital curatorship has become a strong feature of museum practice in which objects displayed in museum collections, that were previously regarded by visitors as symbols of inaccessibility, become accessible by virtue of their presence on a digital platform.

Some scholars agree that one way of re-organising knowledge is by encrypting or digitising it, so that it can be accessible. However, according to new media scholar and curator Christiane Paul (2008:3), "new technology challenges the underlying basis of the traditional museum by inducing a shift in long-established, institutionalised practices, such as customary methods of presentation and documentation, as well as its approach to the collection and preservation from a spatially pre-determined to a digitally-informed orientation." Elaborating on how museums and galleries themselves have been predicated by forms and practices of "objectification", Paul (2008:3) asserts that "ongoing developments in digital and information technologies will affect the nature and structure of cultural institutions in the coming decades." However, the use of digital technology in a museum has become an interesting strategic tool, offering new possibilities for the online storage, preservation, and documentation of cultural objects, whilst assuming a large-scale mediating responsibility.

However, Finney and Burnard (2007:110) remain convinced that "digital curatorship has progressed from a state of adopting digital processes and platforms to one of wider digital integration or adaptation occurring across organisations, whether embedded in strategic and operational policies or naturalised through various museological practices, including modes of curating."

2.4.1 Digital curatorship

The term "digital curatorship" was first used in 2001 to embrace "digital preservation, data curation, and the management of assets over their lifecycle" (Lee, Tibbo & Schaefer, 2007:50). After many attempts to define digital curatorship, the term is still defined differently by different people. However, digital curatorship generally speaks to a "diversity of stakeholders and environments in which it is conducted and potentially involves anyone who interacts with digital information during its lifecycle" (Poole, 2016:3).

Fleckner (1991) expresses concern about the role of digital curation professionals, because it is a role performed by a variety of people who undertake varied tasks in different settings. Consequently, digital curatorship "work may seem mundane or even invisible and as such, neither the demand nor the impact of curation activities can easily be measured" (Poole, 2016:3).

Domínguez (2014) points out that traditionally, digital curatorship takes a more holistic view in the circulation of information by recognising it as collective intellectual impulse, which contributes to the development of a society, whereas the most basic assumption is that digital curation implies not only preservation and maintenance, but also adds some sense of meaning and knowledge production.

As a result of digital proliferation, the physical degradation of museum collections must be carefully controlled in order to preserve their intelligibility as meaningful and valuable cultural objects (DeSilvey, 2006). Just like any other physical material, cultural objects are subject to entropic processes of degradation and decay. Cameron (2007) explains that digital curatorship entails a balanced combination of the physical analogue and digital objects commonly bound by an analogue counterpart, bonds that are not necessarily characteristic of the physical object.

Put differently, all museum objects undergo a continual process of physical transformation and decay that constantly threatens to undermine the specific relationship between the material form, and the intention that defines them as meaningful and valuable objects. The question that "museums have to resolve is how to prevent, or at least how to slow down, this unremitting process of change and degradation so that cultural objects can retain their meaning and value as timeless objects of formal delectation, which requires a vast material and technological infrastructure" (Domínguez, 2014:17).

The term "digitisation" causes confusion because it tends to isolate technology from its historical development through media and related practices (Kress & van Leeuwen, 2001:90). For example, technology in museums is not necessarily that new. The history of modern museums coincides with the emerging history of technology. The new media technologies of the late nineteenth century did not outmode the museum, but developed the museum project (Henning, 2005:74).

The reawakening of interest in cultural objects managed through technological information has meant that digital curatorship has brought to the fore another way of seeing things. Digital curatorship concerns itself with the "planning and management of digital assets over their lifetime, from conceptualisation, through active use and presentation, to long-term preservation for future use" even though the rate of digital technology's innovation is outpacing the capacity for change in cultural institutions (Akinwale, 2012:16).

2.5 Digitisation and digital preservation

In modern practice, the use of the terms "digitisation" and "digital preservation" are as numerous and sometimes contradictory as the use of "digital curation", so it is not easy to grasp their proper meaning or what essentially separates them (Conway, 2010). Harvey (2005:93) observes that "such terms have been used interchangeably to describe the characteristic elements of digital objects that must be retained for long-term preservation."

Digital preservation and digitisation are developing fields, and are a complex and resource-intensive undertaking (Van Malssen, 2012:13). Kalusopa and Zulu (2009:99) define "digital preservation as a series of adapting management activities necessary to ensure continued access to digital materials for as long as necessary." Asogwa (2011:4) defines "digitisation as the process by which analogue contents are converted into a sequence of 1s and 0s to be readable by a computer. The result is the presentation of an object, image, sound, document or signal usually an analogue signal by generating a series of numbers that describe a discrete set, its points or samples."

The logical end of digitisation is, presumably, to preserve, but for some, digitisation is being touted as a "panacea" for preservation and accessibility challenges (Britz & Lor, 2004:216). Conway (2010:64) sates that digitisation must not be confused with digital preservation and that "it is important to establish clear distinctions between the term digitisation and digital preservation." In a way, digital preservation should be viewed as a progressive tool that enables data preservation and long-term access to digital objects by providing faster and easier access to records. However, Thibodeau (2002:9) reminds us that the notion of digital preservation is not so much to "retrieve" the object as to "reproduce" the same manifestation, and to ensure that the information transferred over time is authentic.

According to some industry insiders, as technology continues to impact on the delivery of information, digitisation is rapidly becoming one of the standards of preservation for public libraries, archives, museums and information centres, where a common requirement for digital preservation is that it should ostensibly guarantee information confidentiality, availability, integrity, authenticity, and that the information's contents are not modified long-term. Routhier (2014:4) states that it is worth recording "something in its original form whenever possible in order to preserve its historical authenticity." This will insulate all types of information contained in an object and give the future generation a better description. According to Manovich (2001:70), although "technology entails the flawless replication of data, [. . .] its actual use in contemporary society is characterised by the loss of data and degradation."

2.6 Classification of cultural objects

This section focusses on the classification of "unknown maker(s)", and the transfer of authorship of rare objects, by highlighting the erasure, or omission, of crucial authorship information from the official museum records. The classification of cultural material is at the heart of language, identity, ownership, and the ethical implications of digitising museum objects. It is important to interrogate the strategies that digital curatorship adopts for classifying nuances and historical biographies when digitising "unknown maker(s)".

The essence of history is to represent the past as well as a future, but European anthropologists, ethnologists and museologists have collected, classified and represented other cultures in a manner that is often perceived with some scepticism. Indeed, most ethnographic and anthropological experts have "failed to identify a single society, which does not bestow personal identities on its members" (Alford, 1988:1). The classification of "unknown maker(s)" cannot be discussed meaningfully outside the context of the socio-political environment in which these objects were created. Many cultural objects find their way into established permanent art collections through acquisition committees comprising industry experts and pundits. ISANG is an example of a cultural institution facing challenges with the classification of its permanent collections. Since the late 1980s, the museum programmes have been overtly concerned with the acquisition of marginalised cultural objects, as well as non-functional and ritual objects, previously regarded as belonging to ethnographic or "tribal" art.

Aside from classifying cultural objects, the need to follow the correct recording procedures cannot be overemphasised. The reliability of digital content is determined by the methods used to generate metadata. In terms of digital curatorship, it is worth noting that the primary function of classifying objects is an essential step in the exhibition of heritage assets in a visual form accompanied by historical biographies or content. An additional consideration is that museum classifications are extremely difficult to change once they have become entrenched in identifying objects.

Besides the classification attributions of museum objects, curation of permanent art collections should not only involve the control of the provenance inventory and access to information about the objects themselves, but should also include managing the data itself as an object. In other words, auxiliary information, such as typology, biography, or geography may assist in uncovering the object's history (Grobler, 2006:36).

The historical evidence of cultural objects is lost over time through various acquired interpretations, observations, aesthetic language, and accumulated knowledge or experiences. The effects of this loss are immeasurable, but may manifest themselves in social dysfunction and alienation that endures for generations (Kreps, 2003:185). As things stand, the current museum metadata gathering methods may leave objects devoid of their original meaning and ultimately cause them to disappear from history.

The power of classification is witnessed in the act of inclusion or exclusion when information pertaining to cultural objects is omitted or erased (Dudley, 2009:9-11). Therefore, digitisation projects are not immune to controversy, data corruption, uncertainty and risk. If museums passively objectify and render cultural makers/creators of rare objects as fictitious by divorcing them from that which they have created, the equality accorded to the "unknown maker" and their art is not a natural reflection of human equivalence, but "rather the result of benevolence" (Van Beurden, 2015:52).

2.6.1 Classification and taxonomies

This section identifies similar studies that have already been undertaken. Additionally, it explores other characteristics of museum culture within the modernist paradigm by highlighting the operating structures that aid in making sense of the world, particularly the imposition of order through systems of museum classification.

Classification is inherently related to categorisation, which is a process in which ideas and objects are recognised, differentiated and understood. We all attempt to make sense of the world "through ordering systems to avoid chaos and to tame the wild profusion of existing things" (Foucault, 1970:15). For example, "we structure the things we possess by applying labels and classifications from the sartorial clues we are presented with and through organisational structures, arranging our record collections according to our preferred classification principles be they alphabetical, chronological, or by genre" (Pearce, 1992:87).

At the most basic level, classification is an everyday phenomenon and its influence is as old as human societies. It is intimately linked with the history of the human race and its mastery over the world. The history of classification may be said to be the same as recording the history of humankind (Nicolaisen, 1976:143).

The essence of classification lies in grouping things together, a compromise between the dynamics of evolution and the stasis of the present (Cowan, 1955:314). Feger (2001:22) suggests that a good classification system has the following criteria (verbatim):

- It has a theoretical foundation that determines the classes and their order.
- The objectivity of such a system allows anybody familiar with the "environment" that is being classified to observe and classify elements in the environment.
- All elements in an environment are represented and have a unique place in the system.
- The simplicity of the system necessitates a small amount of information to establish the system and identify an object.
- The values of variables not used for classification can be predicted, as well as the existence of relations and of objects hitherto unobserved. Thus, the validity of the classification system itself becomes testable.

Kress (2010) and Bowker and Star (1999) point out that classification is an intensely political activity and very much related to selection and recontextualisation. Once classification systems are established, anything that does not fit into a category is likely to either fall through the cracks of recognition and become "othered" or to be mutilated or torqued (Bowker & Star, 1999:223) until it resembles something that meets the conventions of a particular category. Bowker and Star (1999:5) suggest that classifications are intrinsically linked to standards, and that each standard and each category valorises certain points of view and silences others. Furthermore, Kress (2010: 122-123) states that "classification stabilises the social world in particular ways, reflecting the social organisation which has produced [it] and which is the constantly innocuous character of classification also helps to make its political effect more effective."

According to Bowker and Star (1999:299), classification systems are "one of the critical processes through which institutions can produce, and sustain, meaning and order. It is through classification that institutions effectively standardise and synchronise actions and meanings across different domains, organise coherent systems of categories, distribute forms of value, and produce univocal and legible objects of knowledge." These activities "are particularly critical in museums as institutions that have within their purview the creation and reproduction of complex taxonomies" (Domínguez, 2014:12).

Bennett (2013:96) argues that

> [the] birth of the museum is coincident with and supplied a primary institutional condition for the emergence of a new set of knowledge such as geology, biology, archaeology, anthropology, and art history. These bits of knowledge became the principal categories that the material culture collected by museums has been fitted into and formed the basis for the disciplines that museum collections have been ordered. Similarly, their distinct modes of assembling objects are still adhered to by many museums.

Classification systems are used by museums to organise knowledge, value, and meaning. However, for decades, classification of cultural material has been an undervalued museum activity "that came to be viewed as a task of secondary importance rather than functioning as a coherent, interrelated system of information, and collection and documentation at many museums devolved into a series of disjointed, poorly integrated filing systems" (Grobler, 2006:36). Therefore, a more nuanced classificatory system of public records from cultural institutions cannot afford to give low priority to digital heritage materials because information gaps will limit public engagement.

Hein (2000:14) maintains that "the taxonomic impulse, sometimes pushed to pathological extremes, not only rescues billions of objects from temporal oblivion but also bestows meaning and value to them and assigns them a place in a quasi-objective order." Since collections are regarded as central and essential to the institution of the museum, it is assumed that museums contain items that can be identified and classified using their accrued taxonomic, aesthetic or historical significance.

Bennet (2013:96-98) states that

> [museum] classifications are better understood as dynamic and open-ended processes contingently unfolding out of the interplay between classificatory principles and the physical properties of the material, they seek to organise. Artefacts, in this sense, are more than mere inert material organised and classified according to external social or cultural principles. They are elements playing a key role in the production of classification and actively shaping how categories are drawn and redrawn, and how different meanings and forms of value are produced and distributed within the museum.

2.6.2 Representation of cultural objects in a museum

One of the challenges examined in current museum literature concerns the classification of rare or unique objects. It is not a coincidence that many of the great national museums were first established in the nineteenth and twentieth centuries, since this was when the concept of national identity was first broadly addressed (Tietz, 2017:15).

The representation of museum objects is a product of observation because when "an object is removed from its place of origin and its context, its significance is reduced and it becomes more reliant on the documentation linked to it" (Bell, 2017:241). However, many cultural records in museums are inaccurate and often lack basic information. In most cases, the information provided in the cultural collection records is largely administrative and descriptive, and includes object attributes such as identification numbers, typological makeup, storage, and the cataloguer's details. This type of information is best for museum inventories, but lacks informative aspects that are vital for research, interpretation and presentation. For example, the anonymity and inconclusive information about some of the cultural objects, remain prevalent in the museum's documentation processes. As a result, these classificatory methods have dehumanised and erased the full measure of their historical biography. In other words, anonymity has managed to preclude any consideration of the individual creative act. Once the artist's or maker's name is established, the act of ascribing identity must be seen to possess, a certain opacity of both origin and intention" (Biebuyck, 1973:7).

As museums continue to provide important information about people's struggles to control their worldview, "cultural objects become proxies for persons and museums do for objects what society has difficulty doing for the people associated with those objects" (Kirshenblatt-Gimblett, 2004:51). Domínguez (1988:21-23) argues that

> social and human scientists need not limit themselves to studying the first or original meaning of the objects that is, to the makers and initial users or to spending all their energies on attempts to reconstruct that early meaning or the archaeology of objects. They should explore the evolution of meaning about the object and the history of the institutional mechanisms that produce and reproduce those meanings.

Although museum practices have evolved over time, displaying unfamiliar cultural objects with inadequate attention to socio-political intricacies often lends itself to inaccurate historical narratives. A study conducted by South African archivist Verne Harris provides a good example of the cultural misrepresentation that underscores the exotic illusions of those who collected and classified historical accounts of indigenous communities. In his article *Archival sliver: power, memory, and archives in South Africa*, Harris (2002:63) supports the idea that a considerable amount has been written about the role of museums and memorials in the construction of post-apartheid identity, explaining that

> [the] apartheid administered memory institutions and heritage endeavours supported apartheid's sanitised grand narrative and the Apartheid State re-engineered and weighted what was remembered by shaping, naming, using and destroying records to

consolidate power, create their own ruling categories, marginalise the "other", or to escape accountability for their actions.

The misrepresentation of historical narratives built on the injustices of the past brings the urgency of addressing the classification anomalies of cultural objects to the fore. As Van Beurden (2015:134) puts it, cultural objects were tamed, acceptable representatives for real people; substitutes which could be displayed, examined and manipulated. In part, they served no other function than to be looked at, muted and masqueraded by the dominant culture. However, Nelson Mandela (1997:1). reminded us that the advent of democracy has provided the opportunity to make sure that our cultural institutions reflect history in a way that respects the heritage of everyone. Unfortunately, if most of the records from cultural institutions are inconsistent and dominated by inconclusive material that speaks from a point of authority, there will inevitably be distortions, omissions and misrepresentations in relation to the information collected.

2.7 Colonisation and museum objects of curiosity

Colonialism itself is deeply preoccupied with boundaries of territory and identity, borders of nation and state, and with it came the proliferation of historical narratives that Africa was a continent waiting to be discovered. This assumption captured the imagination of many in the Western world wanting to discover the "unknown" about Africa through their colonial expeditions. Colonialism paved the way for a growing interest in, and development of, a large audience for culture in the form of literature, music, art and scientific studies.

As a result, museum objects were exhibited in exclusive settings, wrested from their producers or users. The museum has come under persistent attack in postcolonial discourse because a museum symbolised the dispossession of land and culture by the dominant group through the rapid acquisition of specimens and objects. Moreover, museum collections are perceived to be constituted from their colonial origins and "it is in their nature to fabricate strangeness, otherness and separateness" (Douw, 2017:1).
The lingering effects and systematic discrimination created by colonialism are still evident in many cultural institutions, giving credence to the historical misrepresentation that has

plagued ethnographic materials over the years, especially in the face of attempts to decolonise museums. These misplaced "representations have evoked condescension from academic observers and elicited little appreciation for any scientific insight and understanding that indigenous knowledge systems might offer" (Semali & Kincheloe, 2002:3).

The expansion of colonialism in the nineteenth century gave rise to the historical attitude and political framework in which ethnographic museums came into being. Consequently, "the museum's intellectual framework and many of its collecting methods were closely bound up with the nature and practices of imperialism" (MacKenzie, 2009:4).

The European colonial worldview enabled colonial powers to see their own culture as both universally valid and as the peak of civilisation. Other cultures were, however, discussed, sampled, represented in encyclopaediae and periodicals, in popular displays and public museums. Where the colonial power prevailed, their authority made a lasting statement, even though what was being represented was not necessarily a true reflection of a non-European experience (Henning, 2005). The long histories behind many European cultural institutions inevitably involved legacies of colonialism and expropriation, where collectable and dispossessed items included objects with complex pasts that were acquired in locations very different from today. As a result, most cultural institutions are now caring for objects with contested ownership and historical authenticity.

Other aspects of colonialism that are relevant to this discussion include its ability to establish cultural superiority by imposing foreign epistemology, suppressing native languages (spoken or written) and creating a cosmetic impression that diminished the vibrant plurality of indigenous cultures. This may partly explain why the development of museum classification terminologies has always appeared to be a slightly external method of identification for Africa. Museums cannot afford to discount the displacement of "African cultural objects from their countries of origin, something which reflects a sort of wholesale cultural piracy on the part of the colonisers" (Martin, 2010:5).

Chapter 3: Methodology

3.1 Introduction

This chapter outlines the research instruments, methods of data collection and the data analysis techniques that were used to achieve the objectives of the study. A discussion of validity and reliability regarding the data collection procedures has also been provided.

3.2 Research approach

Denzin and Lincoln (2011:3) explain that "a research methodology or strategy is determined by the nature of the research question being investigated." This study adopted a data triangulation case study strategy, in which, according to Denzin (2006), multiple perspectives of the same phenomenon can be considered through different data sources. This method was adopted because it was best suited to the research problem and provided the flexibility to assess the relevant literature on the topic as well as the comments made by respondents.

According to Hakim (1987:63), "the idea of utilising triangulation in social and behavioral sciences originated In the 1950s." However, despite its advantages, it is not standard practice. Although there are various definitions of data triangulation, "it can be understood as a multifaceted research method that uses multiple theoretical perspectives, procedures, methods, sources of data or investigations to collect and interpret data about a phenomenon" (Brink, 2003:215). The different procedures are used because "the flaws of one are often the strengths of another [and] by combining procedures or techniques, the researcher can utilise the strengths of each, while overcoming their unique deficiencies" (Denzin, 1978:244). But the threats to triangulation validity can influence the research study and design, which potentially include instrumentation, researcher bias and selection of participants (Marczyk, DeMatteo, & Festinger, 2005).

The researcher opted to use a triangulation method because of its ability to provide rich explorations and descriptions of data (Mentz, 2012:126). The adopted method was also chosen because it reinforced an understanding and interpretation of the meaning, as well as possible intentions underlying human interaction within a specific context.

Using a case study is consistent with the activity of triangulating data using two or more techniques, allowing the researcher to uncover different dimensions of the same phenomenon. The evidence produced by different techniques or procedures was compared in order to reveal similarities and incongruencies (Weyers, Strydom & Huisamen, 2008:208).

A triangulation approach can enhance the validity of a case study by developing a holistic picture of the phenomenon in question. The study developed analytic questions and key themes in one dataset and followed these across other methods to generate several datasets in order to create a collection of findings that could be used to generate a multi-faceted picture of the phenomenon. All the datasets alongside each other were positioned conceptually as a thread, "an iterative process of data interrogation which aims to interweave the findings that emerge from each dataset. The value of this integrative analytic approach lies in allowing an inductive lead to the analysis, preserving the value of the open, exploratory, qualitative inquiry but incorporating the focus and specificity of the quantitative data" (Moran-Ellis et al., 2006:16). Therefore, it was felt that the adopted strategy, which works across multiple sources of data, would offer greater variety in the collected data and a more nuanced account of how data converged with each other.

3.3 Ethical considerations

This study made use of an online questionnaire. In designing the research instrument for this study, the researcher was cognisant of ethical considerations such as confidentiality, anonymity, explaining and obtaining informed consent, consulting relevant authorities, and avoiding any possible harm to participants. The researcher obtained ethical clearance from the University of Cape Town, where the researcher was registered at the time of conducting the study, and permission from the research site, to investigate the curatorial context used to develop exhibitions as well as the biographies of objects on display, and how objects are selected, labelled, cased, arranged, represented, and interpreted.

The participants were informed of the research objectives and asked to sign a letter of consent (Appendix A) before participating in the online questionnaire (Appendix C). The researcher also ensured that participants were aware that their participation was voluntary, that they could withdraw from the research at any stage without any ramifications, and that they could choose to leave questions unanswered if they were uncomfortable with answering them.

3.4 Data collection

This study used a variety of research strategies and triangulated data from different sources to enhance the validity and plausibility of the study. Data was gathered as outlined below.

3.4.1 A case study

A defining characteristic of case study research is the ability to use a combination of methods to collect data. Case studies are used regularly in the social sciences and there is confidence that they constitute "a rigorous research strategy in their own right" (Hartley, 2004:323). For instance, ISANG, as a case study, encompasses a wide range of research material which is seen as part of an evolving contemporary museum. Bonoma (1985:202) offers a persuasive argument in favour of the use of case studies in the social field, stating that "many issues of interest to postcolonial scholars of cultural studies and sociology in the social field cannot be studied outside the context in which they naturally occur."

In recognition of the multifaceted nature of data triangulation, "a case study inquiry typically addresses the technically distinctive situation in which there will be many more variables of interest than data points, [with one] result rel[ying] on multiple sources of evidence" (Fouché et al., 2011:148).

3.4.2 Online questionnaire

The online questionnaire, formulated for the targeted population, was informed by the objectives set out at the commencement of this study. The questions were premised on the understanding that museum curatorship, as a profession, requires a knowledge of historical precedents and processes, and the implications of these on the present, and a thorough understanding of cataloguing and classifying museum objects. Additionally, the thematic sets of questions were designed based on their potential to yield the most information about the topic, and it was expected that variations in the answers would bring different issues to light (Leedy & Ormrod, 2005:145).

An online questionnaire comprising closed and open-ended questions was used to collect information from professionals employed by Iziko Museums. Consenting participants were invited to answer an online questionnaire sent to them via email (Appendix B).

An online questionnaire is defined "as an instrument that consists of set questions or other types of prompts that aims to collect information from a respondent. These typically are a mix of close-ended questions and open-ended questions" (Mentz, 2002:21). However, an open-ended questionnaire is one of the most common types of questionnaire, which allows for the collection of data to measure a problem without a predetermined set of responses. In most cases, questionnaires are classified as a quantitative data collection instrument, but in this study an online questionnaire was designed to create a platform that would solicit predominantly qualitative data in the most complete and accurate way possible.

Before sending out the questionnaire, the researcher obtained informed consent from the participating museum professionals. The online questionnaire (Appendix C/ hyperlink: https://trn-redcap.uct.ac.za/surveys/?s=8XXMNJPEC9) was sent to employees selected on the criteria of their level of responsibility and duties at Iziko. The respondents' answers were later transcribed to capture the key themes and points that emerged from the survey. The use of questionnaires is "considered essential in gathering honest and accurate data since questionnaires facilitate the greatest possible anonymity" (Mentz, 2012:101).

However, there are several disadvantages associated with the use of online questionnaires, such as a low response rate and that they are likely to gather unintended responses if the questions are biased. The dependability of the questionnaire was established by linking the findings with other sources, as well as by asking questions in the least ambiguous way.

3.4.3 Purposive sampling

The researcher opted for an informant selection tool, which included museum professionals who were key custodians actively involved in the daily operations of the museum, such as senior collection managers, curators, registrars, archivists, educators, display technicians and directors (Appendix D).

Purposive sampling, also known as judgmental sampling, includes people or items with the characteristic one wishes to understand. As noted by Bernard (2002:23-24), "the purposive sampling technique, is the deliberate choice of an informant due to the qualities and expertise the informant possesses." It is a non-probability technique and is most effective for the study of a certain cultural domain with experts. Alternatively, "a purposive sampling method may prove to be effective when only limited numbers of people can serve as primary data sources due to the nature of research design objectives" (Bernard, 2002:23-24).

The study used a purposive sample of 200 museum professionals selected for their potential to yield the most information about the topic (Leedy & Ormrod, 2005). These individuals were also selected based on the researcher's perception of their skills and expertise in complex curatorial matters such as the acquisition procedures, digitising and management of electronic records, knowledge about art collections management, maintenance of inventory systems, cataloguing of cultural objects, accessioning and treatment of heritage assets under the care of the museum, as well the installation and removal of exhibitions.

3.4.4 Summary of population and sample size

A purposively selected sample of museum professionals from Iziko's Art Collections Department was invited to participate in the online questionnaire. Participants were invited to contribute by email, with a maximum of two additional email reminders sent to participants who had not responded within two weeks. The study achieved an 85% response rate (170 valid responses) from 200 selected Iziko museum professionals, with only 15% (30 responses) being invalid. However, it is also "reasonable to expect that any survey that samples a population or that achieves only a sample by way of respondents will incur some sampling error and possibly sample bias" (Dillman, 2001:206).

3.4.5 Document analysis

The study also made use of document analysis, sometimes referred to as content analysis, which is "a systematic procedure for reviewing and evaluating both printed and electronic materials" such as those published in the ISANG collections policies, annual reports, website, emails, memoranda, ethnographic journals, documentation on displaying exhibitions, and includes studying curatorial material such as collections manuals, catalogue cards and exhibition labels on the individual items that provide a description of the objects and their biographies.

Hall and Rist (1999:297) observe that "what people say is not always what they do, hence document analysis aims to cover this anomaly by compensating for any weaknesses in the online questionnaire." According to Bowen (2009:27), "document analysis is defined as a systematic procedure for reviewing and evaluating both printed and electronic materials as well as verbal or visual communication." The benefits of using document analysis in research includes cost-effectiveness, lack of obtrusiveness and reactivity, and stability in the research data (Bowen, 2009:31).

Collecting data by studying documents follows a similar approach to conducting interviews or observations. Document analysis enabled the researcher to extract key themes, strategies, values and messages from the information stored in sources such as published annual reports, archival records, exhibition reports, policy documents, catalogues, letters, press and media reviews.

In this study, document analysis allowed the researcher to review relevant documents from the year in which the Iziko Digitisation and Art Collections Department was established. The data collected was transcribed and categorised in terms of research questions or themes. The specific themes that guided the collection of documented material included digitisation and collection management, acquisition of collections, access provision, preservation, provenance and classification. These themes were further refined during the data coding, and only information that dealt with the identified themes was used for reporting in this study.

Exhibition visits and assessment of ISANG catalogues records was supported by the taking of comprehensive notes and photographs, which documented pertinent issues around the complexities of museum classification and the incompleteness of information from the museum records and the ethical or digital implications of cataloguing "unknown maker(s)" of cultural objects.

Data derived from organisational documents such as the Iziko digitisation policy and 2003/4 annual report for the period prior to the case study were used to develop a description of the institution and its permanent collection history. In addition, the online survey was statistically evaluated and the convergence of information between organisational documents and questionnaire responses was compared in order to reveal similarities, contradictions or contact points.

3.4.6 Exhibition review

ISANG is a cultural institution with exhibition functions that collect, document, disseminate, and preserve museum objects of cultural significance and perform research and interpretation activities. The ISANG permanent art collections have real objects on-site, which offer real-life context and insight into the vast range of aesthetic products within the South African museum, the African continent and further afield. For the purposes of this study, an active exhibition review offered a unique opportunity for the researcher to obtain reliable data from a curated exhibition.

Although ISANG welcomes the use of its collections for scholarly research, the researcher had to obtain written permission to gain access to the museum's art collection. With the assistance and technical support of senior curators, art collection managers and education officers, the researcher was able to ensure that the best museum practices and guidelines were upheld during the study.

During the exhibition review, cultural objects were listed, and the problems related to classification were explored. This was done so that the researcher understood the curatorial decision-making processes and practices underpinning what information or content was being disclosed in relation to "unknown maker(s)" of cultural objects.

Some of the characteristics of the exhibition reviews included the basic curatorial context used for developing an exhibition as well as the biographies of objects on display — how objects were selected or classified, labelled, cased, arranged, represented, and interpreted through interactive panels or devices, etc.

3.5 Data validity and reliability

The multi-method strategy permitted "the triangulation of data across the inquiry techniques and yielded different insights. The use of combined instruments for collecting data offers a means of validating the data collected" (Guion, Diehl & McDonald, 2011:1).

The use of triangulation as a tool that provides better insight and understanding of a phenomenon or occurrence by "corroborating one source and method with another" (Fouché et al., 2011) has received some criticism because "the convergence gained through triangulation never results in data reduction, but rather in the proliferation of meanings that are brought about by different viewpoints" (Erlandson et al., 1993:139). However, according to Stake (1995:12) "triangulation provides confirmation and allows researchers to obtain a more complete, holistic and contextual portrayal and reveal the varied dimensions of a given phenomenon, with each source contributing an additional piece to the puzzle."

Data retrieved using multiple methods permits triangulation of data across the inquiry techniques to yield different insights by accessing different facets of the same occurrence. More importantly, as data converge, "strong data similarities could be viewed as a validation of the data or conclusions, while incongruencies could be indicative of either one or more faulty procedures or data sets. In the latter case, triangulation provides scope for further analysis of the data or additional exploration and research" (Weyers et al., 2008:208).

3.6 Summary

This chapter presented the rationale for using multiple data sources. It also discussed the procedures that were followed to access various data sets/units, ethical considerations and the reliability of the research. It was important for this study to draw its data from multiple sources in order to capture the complexity of the phenomenon under study. As for the research instruments used to gather data, Yazan (2015:142) "advocates for the combination of quantitative and qualitative evidentiary sources because of both methods ability to converge data in a triangulating fashion and benefit from prior development of theoretical propositions to guide data analysis and collection."

Chapter 4: Data Analysis and Presentation of Findings

4.1 Introduction

This chapter presents evidence collected from ISANG's permanent art collections regarding the classification of "unknown maker(s)" of cultural objects, and uncovers some of the challenges related to classification in the context of a national museum.

4.2 Data analysis approach

The different data collection methods and the triangulation of data used in this study made it possible to collate data and to interpret and represent it using various themes. The various stages of data collection that supplemented the questionnaire data are discussed in the following subsections: Content analysis, Iziko Museums' online presence, Archive-based records, and Exhibition review.

4.2.1 Content analysis

The collated data from the state-funded art institution ISANG offered first-hand information which was used to investigate the digital classification phenomenon of "unknown maker(s)" of cultural objects. In order to gain new insight into the content that was analysed from ISANG permanent collection.

Figure 4.1: *Iziko South African National Gallery, image downloaded 7 September 2018 (https://www.iziko.org.za/).*

4.2.2 Iziko Museums' online presence

Whilst other cultural institutions grapple with emerging digital technologies, the Iziko website presents a summary of activities that the organisation has embarked on over the years. Amongst these is a detailed digitisation policy (Appendix E) that identifies the digitisation of its art collections as a key strategic objective that promotes cultural diversity, social cohesion and accessibility by taking stock, assessing and implementing the museum's art collection management policies.

In the above-mentioned policy, the Iziko digital assets and its publicity material are meant to optimally promote the museum through the internet and augment physical museum visits. But, at a very practical level, the museum leverages its rich digital content to benefit the society at large by making use of digital and online media platforms to ensure that the impact of its collections extends beyond local audiences, to national and international audiences. Based on interactions with the museum's website, information is stored in a standardised form and is systematically retrievable by providing a context within which the organisation and individual artworks can be appreciated more fully, as the museum assumes the responsibility of promoting its art collection to a larger audience.

Another observation made in relation to Iziko's website is the insufficient information available about "unknown maker(s)" in the museum's online catalogue. The digitised museum objects should be preserved over time, especially when limited information is transferred from its original format to a new updated format, and proper procedures should be followed to provide the correct documentation. When digital objects are presented on online, they should at least have the same intrinsic requirements that the original artefact or master copies have. In other words, the important information required by a museum professional to transfer, store, process, and preserve files, which allows a user to retrieve the desired information, should apply both to analogue and digital objects. Thus, "it is important for digital curation to preserve with authenticity, [. . .] the source of the object, establish where the object originates from, whom it came from, and in what context it was created" (Routhier, 2014:2).

Evidently, the Iziko website has insufficient information about "unknown maker(s)" of cultural objects because the relevant information is not being made available online, which does not assist a museum with attracting online visitors. Ultimately, museum goers must be motivated to visit the museum and the website must function as a bridge that connects their pre- and post-visit activities, by helping them learn more about the museum and its collections.

4.2.3 Archive-based records

The acquisition of cultural objects is an important museum practice for ISANG, which houses many works of great cultural significance and historical importance, including examples of the best possible aesthetic quality.

The research considered the museum's official acquisition processes, and acquisition policy documents, which were obtained from the ISANG archives. ISANG's art acquisition committee's terms of reference (Appendix F) highlight important prescripts and criteria for the acquisition of artworks through representation, purchases, commissions, bequests and donations. Although ISANG is perceived as an institution with a high level of adherence to acquisition procedures and management of its art collections, some of its acquisition processes have come under scrutiny. For example, ISANG's inability to apply its art acquisition policy retrospectively, which states that objects without accurate descriptive documentation or provenance cannot be formally introduced into the permanent collections. But there exists a range of aesthetic production in ISANG's care whose provenance is not necessarily accurately documented or easy to identify.

Nonetheless, ISANG has one of the largest and continuously expanding African art collections in the country. One of the exhibits is a pair of engraved Nguni cow horns depicting a scene from the Anglo-Zulu War c. 1879 (Figures 4.2 – 4.5 below). This exhibit provides an example of cultural object makers being described as "unknown". Tracing the Nguni horns through their acquisition files provided invaluable evidentiary data that uncovered some inconsistencies around how indistinct cultural object makers are portrayed and represented by the national museum.

According to the *2003 - 2004 Iziko Annual Report* (2003-2004) (Appendix G), the two horns were repatriated to South Africa by the South African Department of Arts and Culture in collaboration with the German government. The two Nguni horns were formally incorporated into ISANG's permanent collection because of their rarity and the sentimental value associated with the historical event.

Figure 4.2: *Hidden Treasures (2017) Unknown artist, Engraved Anglo-Zulu War of 1879 Nguni cow horns on display, curated by Carol Kauffman, ISANG permanent collection.*

ARTIST	TITLE	MEDIUM	PERIOD & DATE	SCHOOL	TYPE	ACC. NO.
Unknown					n. nguni	

SIZE	
STRETCHER	
FRAME OR BASE	
PHOTOS	
PROVENANCE	
DATE OF ACQUISITION	
BIBLIOGRAPHY COMPARATIVE DATA COLLECTIONS EXHIBITIONS RESTORATION	SEE INSIDE

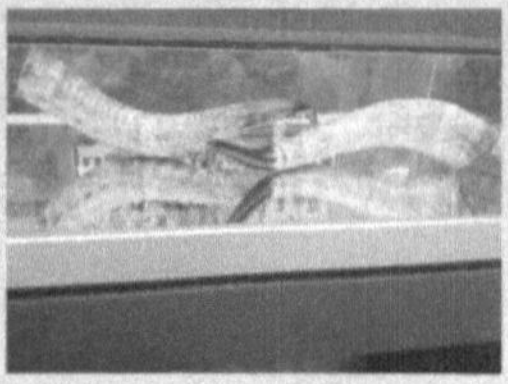

Figure 4.3: ISANG (2019) Digitised acquisition file from ISANG museum archives.

INVENTORY No. INVENTARIS Nr.		LOCATION PLEKAANWYSING
2003/13	ARTIST Unknown KUNSTENAAR	
BOARD-MEETING DATE RAADSVERGA- DERING DATUM	SUBJECT AND DESCRIPTION Nguni horn ONDERWERP EN BESKRYWING	
	INSCRIPTION AND DATE INSKRIPSIE EN DATUM	PHOTOGRAPH NEG. No. FOTO NEG. Nr.
PRICE PRYS	PROCESS MEDIUM	
	SIZE GROOTTE	ENTERED BY INGESKRYF DEUR
INSURANCE VERSEKERING	SOURCE BRON	
NCV 4129	CONDITION ON RECEIPT AND SUBSEQUENT TREATMENT TOESTAND BY ONTVANGS EN DAAROPVOLGENDE BEHANDELING	

Figure 4.4: ISANG (2019) Nguni horns inventory/catalogue card from ISANG museum archives.

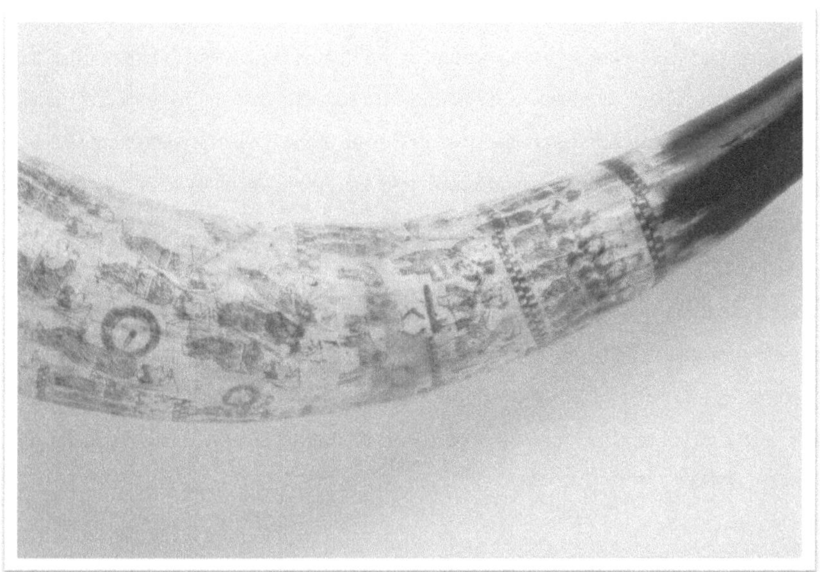

Figure 4.5: *ISANG (2019) Image of Nguni accessioned 2003/13 and 2005/120 from ISANG museum archives*

Apart from the incised motifs chronicling the defeat of the British colonial army by the Zulu nation, the Nguni horns are permanently marked with unique accession numbers (ISANG 2003/13 and ISANG 2005/120) because accessioning is an important procedure that gives an object status in a museum. However, several of the 100 official museum catalogues and inventory cards assessed contained incomplete information. The above example demonstrates the paucity of supplementary information that was recorded specifically regarding the maker of the object. The prevalent use of the "unknown maker" descriptive metadata comes across as an unconscionable reproduced narrative, reminiscent of decontextualised objects being seen as curious pieces, whose main attraction is their exotic origin, and which are separated from their utilitarian function or creator. The absence of basic metadata to describe, attribute and provide context for the "unknown maker(s)" from the official museum catalogue cards is indicative of a lack of local keywords or sophisticated vocabulary for the digital profiling and classification of indeterminable authors of rare objects.

The prevalence of the "unknown maker(s)" label was recently noted at one of ISANG's exhibitions. Of the 92 listed artworks present at the *Hidden Treasures* exhibition, 64 of the catalogue's cards had incomplete information. This suggests that the biographical details about the unknown object makers had been neglected, since the ascribed notations on the catalogue cards were arbitrary, and could also be indicative of established museum orthodoxies of presenting and classifying heritage assets.

It appears that the museum has not yet managed to create a balance between recording accurate information and using the conceptually flawed term "unknown maker" to denote indistinct cultural object makers, which raises serious questions about how the museum deals with cultural objects made by people who do not necessarily subscribe to formal museum settings.

Cultural objects, like descriptive text, can be read as historical documents and interpreted differently in different contexts. The term "unknown maker" merely confirms the possible discrepancies in the museum inventory register, which is the source of basic information for each museum object. However, if a museum catalogues cultural objects in ways that cause neither confusion nor offense by using local vocabulary or keywords for classification purposes and as a guide for identifying accurate sources that provide primary information about the history and biographies of object makers, museum classification and categorisation will have more value for later generations and perhaps even carry out the creator's original intent.

4.2.4 Exhibition review

An exhibition review is a unique conceptual instrument that can be used to visually analyse different aspects of profiling "unknown makers" of cultural objects, as well as how the arrangement and placement of these objects in the overall ISANG classification system can affect their meaning.

A recent long-term exhibition curated by former senior curator Carol Kauffman was used for the review. The exhibition titled *Hidden Treasures* was installed in galleries 10 and 11 at ISANG and introduced African objects that have not been displayed for over 20 years. The exhibition largely comprised an eclectic mix of rare works of art originating from the Southern African region, including Central and West Africa, that were grouped in a coherent and thematic setting representing basic examples of non-Western art forms. The curatorial approach sought to celebrate the unique qualities of innovation, virtuosity and originality that define little known artworks as ethnography.

According to the exhibition's introductory text, the exhibition was configured around the divide between classical art and "tribal art" which remains contested in the field of African art history. Moreover, the exhibition foregrounds the treatment of "unknown maker(s)" who created complicated objects and how the museum presents art made for reasons unfamiliar to the audience and remote from the museum's purposes.

At the time of reviewing the exhibition, approximately 64 "unknown maker(s)" of cultural objects were listed in the *Hidden Treasures* exhibition, highlighting an occasion where the majority of cultural practitioners were classified with the "unknown maker" term (see in situ photographs in Appendix H). The exhibition also presented the curatorial gaze that exists when displaying a variety of "unknown maker(s)" of cultural objects with caricatured identities reflecting how contested museum classificatory systems remain unexplored in modern curatorship.

As a point of entry, the African mask symbolises a tool that assists us with understanding the African artists who are masters of their craft in expressing their worldview and artistic concepts. The iconic African mask carries with it the typology best recognised as a poignant example for representing Africa, which is often viewed as nothing more than a product of archaic technology.

Figure 4.6: Hidden Treasures (2017) Masks exhibition installation curated by Carol Kauffman, Masks bequeathed by Mr. Max Leipold, ISANG permanent collection.

Figure 4.7: Hidden Treasures (2017) Unknown maker, Feminine guardian of the initiation camp/Ivory Coast: Ceremonial mask, ISANG permanent collection.

Figure 4.8: Hidden Treasures (2017) Unknown maker label, Ivory Coast, Dan/Bete-Guro people: Ceremonial mask, Mid-20th century, ISANG permanent collection.

Figure 4.9: Hidden Treasures (2017) Unknown maker, Ceremonial mask, Ivory Coast/Dan people/ N'Guere or Bete, ISANG permanent collection.

A small group of African masks, bequeathed by Mr. Max Leipold for the *Hidden Treasures* exhibition, was selected for an in-depth classification analysis (Appendix I). The African mask exemplifies the disjunction between the classification of objects as classical art and "tribal" art, especially with regards to the curatorial treatment and referencing of non-Western objects as opposed to traditional classical fine art objects.

At first glance, the most striking thing about the indiscriminately mixed masks, shown in Figure 4.6, is the great aesthetic appeal and skilful handling of materials by the ingenious artists/craftsmen. However, exhibiting indistinct African masks is not without its risks as most of them are not attributed to a particular maker or creator. This anonymity seems to suggest that displaying the names or social status of the creative individuals was difficult because of a lack of available information.

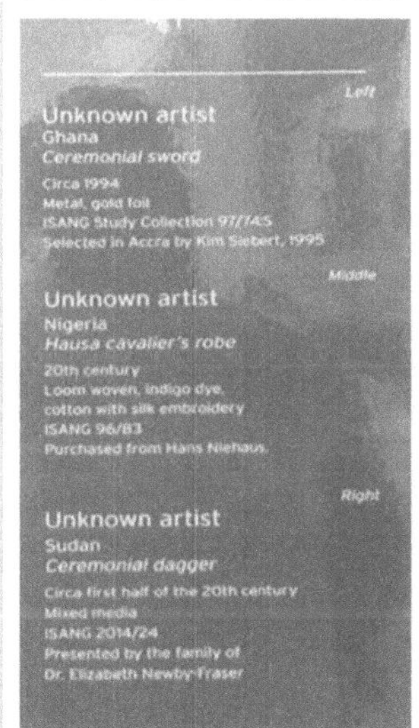

Figure 4.10: *Hidden Treasures (2017) Unknown maker label, Ghana ceremonial sword, Nigeria Hausa cavalier's robe: Sudan ceremonial dagger, Mid-20th century, ISANG permanent collection.*

Figure 4.11: *Hidden Treasures (2017) Unknown maker label, Girl's apron, 20th century, ISANG permanent collection.*

Based on the minimal contextual labelling used at the exhibition as shown in (Figures 4.10 – 4.11), it would appear that the disproportionate display of incomplete information regarding the maker/creator as an agent of cultural production is circumscribed by the need to fit into an established system of classification influenced by conventional museum standards. More importantly, the otherwise "unknown maker(s)" underscore how the system of ordering things that once served as evidence for cabinets of curiosity appears to be a reflection of the limited interest in collecting or disseminating information or knowledge regarding non-Western cultural objects.

The number of incomplete and unresolved ISANG catalogue records suggests that the information offered about the cultural objects does not often hint at the creator or socio-political concerns of the time. At the level of engagement with the visitors, the *Hidden Treasures* exhibition generated an interesting mix of views that went beyond the conflicting "unknown maker" classificatory attributions. However, ISANG must consider that its cataloguing and classification of "unknown maker(s)" of cultural objects might elicit a limited historical interpretation and understanding about the collection under its care.

4.3 Data presentation

The data was collected using a systematic approach to organising data narratives for a descriptive analysis, where an array of data was evaluated and contrasted to meet the research objectives discussed in Chapter One. The data revealed some of the curatorial and practical challenges concerning how "unknown marker(s)" of cultural objects are classified in practice, and the particular role that identity plays in this process, by highlighting some of the institutional inadequacies which may exist in relation to digital curatorship.

4.3.1 Description of data collection

The online questionnaire was administered 1 October to 30 November 2019. The REDCap software web tool was used to transcribe the results by generating a descriptive analysis. The first set of questions (1 to 4) asked about core functions in the museum, which required the museum professionals to explain their responsibilities within the museum environment. The second set of questions (5 to 9) was concerned with art collection management and asked about the processes involved in profiling, classifying and exhibiting Iziko's permanent art collection. The final set of questions (10 to 15) asked the respondents about Iziko's digitisation policy and how the museum provides information about context, provenance and authorship for digital objects, especially when the information is not made available.

At the time of collecting data, an overall response rate of 20 % (± 47 responses) was expected, and responses were considered valid if participants answered at least 80 % of the questions in addition to the three multiple-choice questions. The online questionnaires, with an error margin of 2.8 %, yielded 200 targeted responses from museum professionals from the Iziko population. Thus, warranting the use of descriptive analysis, the results of which are presented for each category below.

4.3.2 Data analysis of questions about core functions in the museum

i.   **Museum responsibilities**

When asked to briefly describe their responsibilities and expertise in the museum environment, 110 (64.7 %) of respondents said that they worked directly with the museum collection and that their occupation, as mandated by the Department of Arts and Culture, required them to prioritise the preservation and safeguarding of the museum's physical objects. More importantly, they had to inspire people to celebrate and respect different cultures by promoting the country's diverse art collections, because unique cultural objects always form part of an irreplaceable museum collection.

ii.   The importance of acquiring artefacts

Senior curators and museum directors indicated that the formation of the Iziko Museums of South Africa should be viewed as an official post-apartheid attempt to demarginalise communities, and as a positive influence on nation building as a result of the curation and interpretation of different cultural material. By extension, the subsidised cultural institution must actively fulfil the necessary function of acquiring objects that reflect the history of the country by using the museum's provisional budget to purchase, commission, and acquire significant objects through representations, loans, bequests and donations.

iii.   Auditing of Iziko's holdings

Figure 4.12 provides a summary of responses from museum professionals who were asked if Iziko had conducted an audit of its holdings for digitisation purposes. The majority of respondents indicated that they were engaged with the management and handling of the art collection in their day-to-day operations. As far as they were aware, the completion of the auditing and evaluation process of Iziko's heritage assets was merely an accounting and compliance process as opposed to the digitisation of heritage assets.

Counts/frequency: Yes N=110   No N= 40   Not sure N= 20

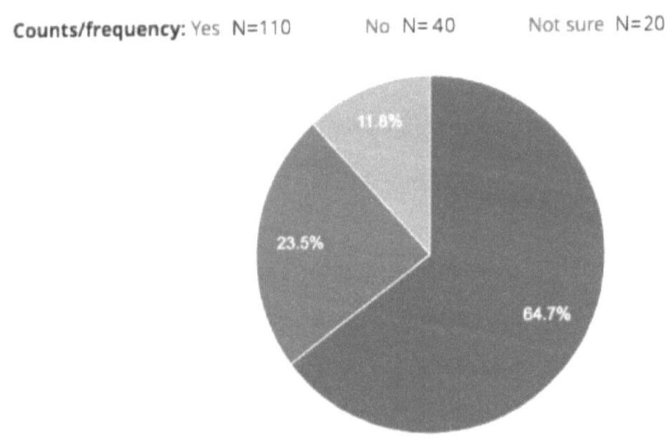

Figure 4.12: A summary of responses regarding the auditing of ISANG's collection

4.3.3 Data analysis of questions about art collections management

i.   Curatorial manual and classification standards

Figure 4.13 summarises the museum professionals' responses to question 5, which asked if a curatorial manual or metadata schema exists for staff members to adopt when classifying national heritage assets. Although, there are various standards to frame data, different curatorial departments have their own established curatorial manuals and classification standards widely accepted by art collection managers for record-keeping purposes. Their museum curatorial manual articulates all of the fundamentals concerning the metadata schema protocols, description syntax and cataloguing of museum objects in line with their various collections under their care.

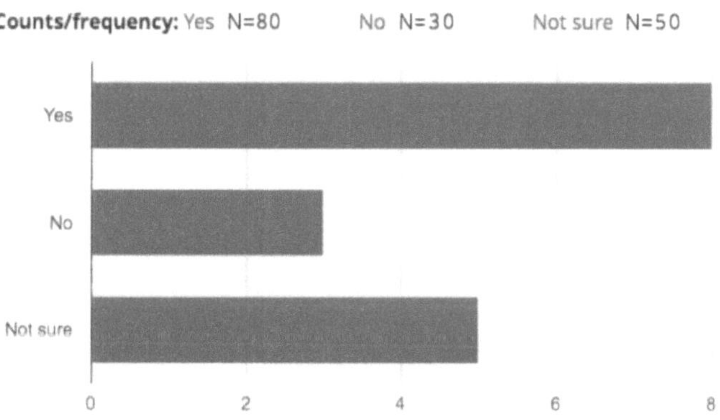

Figure 4.13: *Responses concerning how ISANG's national heritage assets are classified.*

ii.   Profiling and classifying processes

Question 6 asked museum professionals to briefly describe the processes involved in profiling, classifying and exhibiting Iziko's permanent art collection, and to discuss any perceived strengths or weaknesses in the system. The Iziko executive management mentioned that art collection managers, curators, researchers, and registrars are responsible for different areas of the museum's functions, and that they are familiar with documenting and classifying the permanent art collections.

However, 80 (50 %) of Iziko's art collection managers, archivists, researchers and registrars described the profiling, classification and exhibition of Iziko's permanent art collections as a process that involves managing and arranging information according to its typology or the physical characteristics expressed by the artist, and the material properties or makeup of the individual object. Each distinct museum object is expected to be accessioned and classified according to its ethnicity and the cultural group which it comes from, the name of the object maker, and how and when it was obtained so that the museum can assume full responsibility for the object. However, some museum professionals, such as curators, are of the view that a much simpler and more straightforward way of classifying a museum object is to register the creator/maker's name, date, and the title of the object without including pertinent facts about its provenance or who made the object in the first place.

iii.   Curatorial strengths

The museum professionals revealed that the most satisfactory method of cataloguing and classifying museum objects is to record them according to their purpose or function using the museum's convention of compiling an inventory card. Each object would then have its historical context catalogued before it is registered or entered into the museum's official records.

iv.   Curatorial weaknesses

The transfer of inauthentic information between metadata systems such as inventory cards and digital repositories was indicated as being a primary weakness by 50 (35.3 %) of respondents. This has been a long-standing issue for the museum resulting from the inadequate classification systems that do not always reflect the identities of object makers. In ISANG's case, the curatorial department responsible for facilitating the classification processes did not always have the capacity to conduct in-depth research on the objects themselves, and they seemed to assume that curatorial decisions were solely based on mediation and interpretation. A population of 50 (75,5%) researchers and art education officers also mentioned that the cataloguing and classification of objects receives little attention, and lack of training for staff.

v. Exhibiting exotic cultures

According to the curator of the African art collection at Iziko, the museum's display methods still arrange objects according to an evolutionary ranking, exhibiting objects of curiosity in a reductive way and reserving prestigious positions in exhibitions for the classical art objects. For example, ISANG's exhibitions have represented a range of visual culture that includes artworks by African artists, as well as historical artifacts, which now take their place alongside more conventional paintings and sculptures in the gallery. But the classification of cultural objects as "unknown maker(s)" still partly denies a nuanced presentation of the object, while the anonymity of the creator denies producers of cultural objects the opportunity to be acknowledged, which is often afforded to artists producing classical art objects.

Addressing the classificatory attributions of "unknown" cultural object makers, and their contested biographies, in a collection of Iziko's size, is a daunting task because the classification principles have changed over time. However, the museum professionals are proactively working with tools at the museum's disposal to deal with the contested biographies or compromised metadata of unknown identities.

vi. Descriptive metadata

Even though some museum professionals have a thorough understanding of both their classification and cataloguing responsibilities 30 (11.8 %) of the respondents felt that in the absence of a controlled vocabulary suitable for expressing incomplete information, anomalous descriptive variables or information gaps would remain in the museum's official records. However, in some cases, museum professionals might not have intended to disengage with the objects' descriptive metadata. Instead, the excluded information accompanying "unknown maker(s)" might have been considered insignificant or contradictory. The director of Iziko mentioned that the metadata attribution method used in the museum shows how different caretakers of the collection used different interventions at different times. It also demonstrates the complexities associated with different curatorial stages of ingesting information about "unknown maker(s)" cultural objects.

vii.   Challenges encountered

Of the art collection registrars surveyed for this study, 40 (23.5 %) felt that cultural objects usually require extraordinary attention in terms of engaging with their basic historical information, because this forms part of the information required by the curator to develop a context for display and exhibition purposes. Taking the complex curatorial relationship between identifying and attributing museum objects into consideration, art collection registrars expressed a number of ongoing challenges regarding the cataloguing of unidentified makers/creators, especially when the names or identities of the object makers were not easily discernible. This might be exacerbated by the identity of the object maker, or by part of the object maker's name being in a language that is not compatible with the current museum taxonomy, or that the object may be so old and rare that the inscribed word(s) from which the identity should be derived are no longer in current use. The identity may also have been so greatly adapted or corrupted that it is no longer recognisable. The choice of classification terms to describe an "unknown maker" or individual, always involves some form of translation, either directly from the vernacular language used by the original owner, or indirectly from the memory of the collector.

4.3.4 Data analysis of digital preservation questions

i.   Digitisation policy

Figure 4.14 provides a summary of the responses from the museum professionals who were asked if Iziko had a comprehensive digitisation policy. The museum executive management suggested that Iziko needs to prioritise a proactive digitisation policy for the preservation and management of its permanent collection as it continues to grow at a considerable rate.

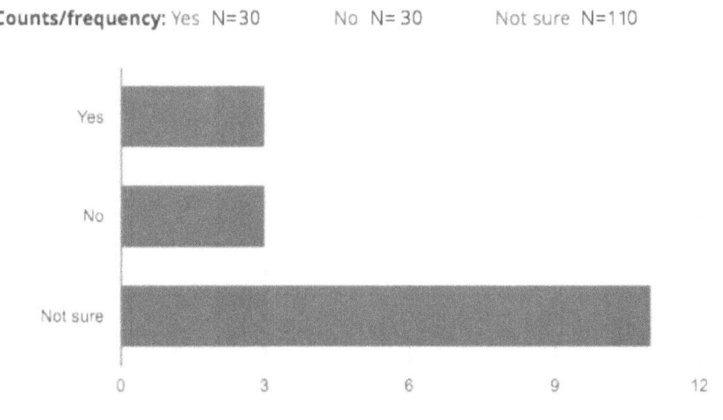

Figure 4.14: *Awareness of the existence of a digitisation policy at Iziko*

There is a perception that digitisation comes with challenges and technical complexities that museum professionals have not yet faced, like the maintenance and updating of digital files. However, 110 (64.7 %) respondents mentioned that they were receptive to, and aware of, the emerging new technology. Having a comprehensive digitisation policy would signal an important step in the museum's next phase of growth, which would have a profound impact on how the museum functions and how it renders its services, by creating a situation where members of the public could interact with artworks. However, as new technological demands emerge, museum professionals remain under pressure to adapt to, and embrace, these new digital changes. Therefore, there is a need for a highly skilled workforce that can meet the requirements of a modern museum.

ii.   Transferring documents and data into digital formats

Museum professionals were asked how Iziko provides information about context, provenance and authorship for digital objects, especially when the information is not available. The museum professionals responses varied but registrars, data captures and archivists indicated that the historical information concerning an object constitutes its provenance. However, in their experience, the perception is that digital records and new technology will immediately solve many of the collection's management challenges even though digital objects are easier to manipulate and that their authenticity is not always apparent. An efficient collections management system can only be accomplished through the effort and commitment of the staff complement in the museum, regardless of the technology available.

iii.   Providing context and provenance

Insofar as providing context and provenance for digital objects is concerned, it is difficult for the curatorial staff to ascertain authorship for cultural objects with incomplete information. As a result, museum objects become displaced, misrepresented and decontextualised in the way that they are exhibited. Another common mistake pointed out by 30 (17.6 %) of ISANG's art collection managers was that if the persons responsible for documenting the collection were vague in their descriptive metadata and did not specify the origins of the museum object at that time, the museum ran the risk of losing information in the process, making it difficult to establish a context in the future.

iv.   Ethical stance regarding the classification of "unknown maker(s)"

Question 12 asked the respondents what they thought the museum's ethical stance and practice was when it came to classifying "unknown maker(s)" of cultural objects. The museum professionals emphasised that when an object/artefact is added to the collection, the museum effectively claims custodianship of the object and, at the same time, alienates it from its owner or maker. However, there are ethical issues with misrepresenting cultural objects such as the use of derogatory terms, information manipulation or the repurposing of digital heritage objects. A museum must ensure that its content is authentic and trustworthy, and that its informational content is not modified in any way because a museum is viewed as an ethical and moral contributor to society. In the context of South Africa, the International Council of Museums code of ethics is endorsed by the South African Museums Association and Iziko Museums of South Africa adheres to this code. Consequently, Iziko Museums' ethical stance is to hold the collection in public trust with an expectation of permanency.

In this regard, the practice of classifying "unknown maker(s)" carries both an ethical obligation and a legal responsibility to establish guidelines that oversee the museum's classification methods. However, 30 (18.8 %) of the curatorial staff members claimed that very little has been done about the long history of cultural objectification, particularly as this pertains to cultural/ethnographic objects that may have been illegally removed from their countries of origin. For instance, there are delicate indigenous objects and relics that are currently on display against the will of their creators and customary users.

According to Iziko museum professionals, the reality that the "museum is legally accountable for the collections in its care means that collections management is much more than a commitment to the general welfare of heritage assets" (Grobler, 2006:38). In a legal sense, it is a mandatory practice that the museum must uphold.

v.   Representation of "unknown maker(s)"

Of the curators, art collection managers and researchers who answered the question, 50 (31.3 %) noted the difficulty with representing cultural objects that have an elusive provenance. A significant number of Iziko's cultural objects have documentation and cataloguing challenges. ISANG's records confirm that some objects are classified as "unknown maker(s)". Implicit in the representation of cultural objects carrying the "unknown maker(s)" description, is the lack of research into authorship, ownership, preservation and representation of indeterminable makers/creators of cultural objects.

Each museum object is representative of specific cultural knowledge, and their meanings can be reinterpreted. Therefore, representing "unknown maker(s)" is only made possible by placing other similar cultural objects together. Museum professionals emphasised that following the basic principles of cataloguing museum objects by including display labels written in multiple vernacular languages, would play a vital role in assisting curatorial staff with circumscribing the objects' potential meaning and create an acceptable meditated representation of the object creator.

vi.   Erasure and omissions of crucial information

Museum professionals did not indicate whether Iziko's approach to cataloguing contributes to the erasure or omission of crucial information from their official inventory. They stated that although classification schema vary across time and space, museum objects and their cataloguing methods could reveal a great deal about the conditions in which they were collected and the reasons for their collection. Errors in naming conventions and negligence in respect of classification standards, sometimes lead to arbitrary attributions to museum objects. This is exacerbated by metadata inconsistencies and a lack of clear documentation processes. Therefore, there are multiple reasons as to why crucial information has been erased and omitted from Iziko's records.

Classification and cataloguing form an integral part of the museum. The "basic system of museum documentation such as catalogue cards and ledgers, function[s] adequately because these [are] supported by a strong framework of oral tradition. In other words, the knowledge and memory of the staff who [have] worked in a museum for many years constitute[s] a considerable wealth of unrecorded history about the museum objects" (Grobler, 2006:40). Admittedly, there are risks in viewing gained experience as a legitimate source of information about museum objects, because museum information should be altered as little as possible in order for it to retain its authenticity.

Museums are expected to be custodians of scientific information, which is extremely difficult to replace once it has been officially catalogued into a repository. It can thus be concluded that this research study highlighted some of the underlying contradictions and provided insight into the curatorial challenges encountered by the Iziko museum professionals. For instance, the triangulated data has shown incongruency in the implementation of a descriptive metadata schema for classifying cultural museum objects as shown in the incomplete inventory cards assessed from the 2017 *Hidden Treasures* exhibition review. In addition, it is interesting to note that even though Iziko museum professionals are familiar with the museum's digitisation prescripts, there exists a lack of adherence to the museum's classificatory standards and inconsistencies in its collection management database. It would be interesting to speculate further about the reasons for profiling makers of cultural objects as an unknown in the ISANG permanent collection. Digitisation is a characteristic phenomenon of the current times, which is most likely to make information reliable and accessible for future usage.

Taking into consideration some of Iziko's appraisal techniques and cataloguing shortcomings, the erasure or omission of people who created the cultural objects from the museum's records brings authenticity sharply into focus. In the absence of an accurate and authentic referencing method for cultural object makers, the term "unknown maker(s)" will continue to be devoid of multiple narratives that acknowledges lived experiences by ignoring the identities of individuals or communities.

4.4 Summary

The data suggests that the classification of "unknown maker(s)" represents a curatorial dilemma, where the inconsistent museum classification term "unknown maker(s)" is used to nullify the identities of people who are inextricably linked to their cultural objects. The data revealed many divergent opinions and positions regarding how cultural objects are classified. This case study, in particular, demonstrates that acquiring cultural objects with historical significance without adequate information has the potential to decontextualise and displace many of the unknown maker(s) of cultural objects within a museum environment, which deserves to be looked at further.

In addition to the treatment of, and insights gained, about the classification of the "unknown maker(s)", this study revealed that museum professionals are well informed and are knowledgeable about cultural objects situated in different museum settings. The study also highlighted how problematic biographical records of cultural objects and museum classification practices leave many of the museum objects in a vulnerable position. The introduction of an inclusive and controlled vocabulary would improve consistency and the reliability of the metadata used in museum classification processes.

It appears that an object preserved without the consent of its creator or maker could potentially keep creators of cultural objects locked into a contentious classification system or unsubstantiated cultural categories because of insufficient information. This is particularly evident when a museum describes object makers as "unknown", which strips the creator of his/her ingenuity, re-enforcing a particular way of ordering, that affects the curatorial ability to present multiple perspectives in rewriting histories of the past.

Chapter 5: Findings, Discussion, Recommendations and Suggestions for Future Research

5.1 Introduction

This chapter discusses important points concerning the classification methods used by ISANG to describe "unknown maker(s)", and the omission of biographical information from their official records, which suggest that the "museum has not familiarised itself with the detailed collection descriptions of its collections" (Davison, 1991:98).

5.2 Findings

The data revealed some of the practical and technical challenges resulting from the potential loss of important information that occurs when digitally preserving and classifying "unknown maker(s)" in a publicly funded art institution. As an institution, ISANG does not have adequate storage space for its growing collection. Digitisation offers a partial solution to this problem, by allowing artworks to be displayed virtually when they are not immediately available for viewing in the gallery. However, an immediate challenge facing ISANG, and its museum professionals, is that once objects are digitised, the new format requires ongoing management because it is easy to manipulate any form of digital representation.

Proper digitisation and preservation strategies are central to documenting cultural objects. However, digital preservation is yet to have a major impact on how museums classify their collections. In the context of ISANG, the regular acquisition of new objects coupled with inadequate storage space, means that the museum should consider starting the digitisation process when it acquires the objects. This would also help avoid the potential loss of important data associated with digital cataloguing.

The digitisation of cultural/heritage objects forms only a small part of digital preservation since digitised museum objects do not necessarily resemble the actual objects themselves, and digitisation does not replace the physical need for object-based encounters. The irony of museums is that although digital formats offer an experience of the "real thing", if they are unmediated, the cultural history and the current context of the objects, including the way of describing the object and its meaning, may be eroded (Hall, 1980: 28).

The data collected from the online questionnaire offered different opinions and ideas about the possibilities of, and obstacles to, profiling and mediating for cultural objects associated with "unknown maker(s)". The research also drew attention to existing curatorial dilemmas regarding how to catalogue cultural objects created by "unknown maker(s)", and the need to consider how to reshape the hierarchies of value regarding people, places and even artistic representation.

As new technologies transform information storage and art collection management procedures, the assertion that museums alone can interpret or discern information from other cultures, presupposes that digital representation of cultural memories, as well as their narratives, will be directly affected by digital curatorship. Digital curatorship bears the responsibility of establishing public trust by becoming a reliable means of preserving information about inaccessible and unique museum objects.

5.3 Discussions

5.3.1 Decolonising museum objects

The postcolonial museological literature in South Africa is confronted with contested ideologies where decolonisation of certain museum collections has gained discursive currency in a transforming society. The visible classification and labelling systems that museums impose on cultural objects have recently come under scrutiny for effectively stagnating indigenous historical accounts, and for obliterating the essential fluidity of non-Western cultural formations or affiliation. Thus, the ambivalent usage of the term "unknown maker(s)" is the subject of debate because it represents a novel strategy that anonymises cultural objects by either disconnecting the artwork from the artist, or by disempowering the very people who know about its history. In effect, the term may be perceived to justify the ordering of things that once served as evidence for objects of curiosity, and sensitivity to such issues cannot be ignored in a preservation system that depends on consistency and authenticity.

The practices that allow for the use of the term "unknown maker(s)" in a museum have effectively denied "the individual genius, that element which more than any other defines enlightenment and modernity, which was reserved for Europeans, while the rest of humanity is identified with the collective, anonymous production pattern that inscribes primitivism" (Oguibe, 2004:14).

As a result, museums face the dual challenge of shaking off their colonial past, and redefining a role in conserving cultures gravely undermined by inconsistent classification methods. As a result of their colonial history many museums continue to present objects in ways that have alienated the objects from the communities that originally produced and used them (Bjerregaard, 2006:21).

The decolonisation process cannot be limited to "deconstructing the dominant story and revealing underlying texts rather decolonisation should be seen as a process of emancipation through mirroring, a mix of defiance and mimesis" (Parekh & Pieterse, 1995: 11). An important milestone in decolonisation is the recognition that museums are not "owners", but are custodians of collections, "with an obligation to preserve the knowledge about people who created the objects" (Howarth, 2018:4).

5.3.2 Museum ethics

Until recently, "works of classical African art were dutifully associated to a tribe rather than to the individual artist, effectively eroding the latter from the narrative spaces of art history" (Oguibe 2004:14). It is as if the term "tribe" guarantees anonymity in the absence of a named creator or author. A persistent challenge facing museums lies in how to identify what is to be digitally preserved. This raises several ethical considerations that include questions about acquisition, funding and the involvement of such institutions in communities.

Overall, the digitisation of heritage materials is a positive aspect of evolving practices, but the real challenges are not technical or technological, they are ethical and sometimes political. A museum should be viewed as an ethical or moral contributor to a society. The question of object ownership, cultural identity, and copyright are some of the most delicate issues concerning new technology's ability to reproduce and disseminate information quickly.

5.4 Recommendations

The increasing demand for instant access to information and the growing digitisation trend require contemporary museums to constantly interpret and reinterpret cultural objects in order to deepen the understanding of the objects kept in their collections (Deliss, 2015:3-4). For instance, despite all of the classification challenges encountered by ISANG, the museum must remain committed to a labelling and classification system that provides reliable information about the identity of the author or creator by focussing on standardising the vocabulary used to describe cultural objects, choosing equipment best suited to the museum environment, offering training to their staff on how to use this equipment and having the means to maintain it (Bjerregaard, 2006).

The insights that emerged from this study broadly support the idea that as new technology expands rapidly cultural institutions, like the Iziko Museums of South Africa, should consider adopting a progressive digitisation policy. Such a policy will improve their services by addressing institutional inadequacies, particularly those related to the technological skills needed to manage digital content generated from digitisation projects and appropriate infrastructure to support information and communications technology.

Iziko's attitude towards the digitisation of cultural objects demonstrates an appreciation for the important role played by digital curatorship. The museum intends to integrate new technologies to profile its permanent collection, and build a long-lasting relationship with its audience by attracting online visitors to the museum's virtual collections, and encouraging them to come to the museum in person. There exists an opportunity for the museum to improve the quality of information throughout its communication platforms and to incorporate the interactive elements of social media through a robust online presence using social networks like Instagram, Twitter and Facebook. It is even possible for a well-designed website to recruit new visitors to a museum, including those individuals who rarely, if ever, visit museums in person.

Should ISANG adopt these measures, it would be in a better position to engage with the process of reimagining how cultural objects, characterised by anonymity, can be represented, while confronting museum classification methodologies that are embedded in the epistemological arrangement of classifying cultural and historical objects.

5.5 Suggestions for future research

This study showed that museums in the twenty-first century have to respond to the increasing demand for authenticity and diversity in representation. Although the introduction of new technologies into museums is encouraging, the use of vernacular languages to represent cultural objects coded in artefacts should be explored further in order to examine the relationship between language and the classification of "unknown maker(s)" of cultural objects. Since language ingenuity is a carrier of identity, revealing who or what we are, those who are denied the opportunity to use their language cannot make their experience known and, therefore, cannot influence the course of their history (Kwesi Kwaa Prah, 2015). Additionally, this study provides some motivation for training museum professionals on how to adequately deal with culturally unique museum objects made by "unknown maker(s)".

5.6 Closing remarks

The objective of this study was to investigate the digital classification of "unknown maker(s)" of cultural objects housed in ISANG's permanent collection using a case study approach. The research explored what precautions a museum could reasonably take to ensure that the digital classification of "unknown" identities does not perpetuate ethically unsound narratives when transferring them from the physical collection into the digital space. The findings confirm the inconsistency regarding the classification of "unknown maker(s)" of cultural objects by providing a critique of the curatorial framework(s) used to digitally profile "unknown maker(s)" of cultural objects.

The material makeup of an individual cultural object provides forensic information and evidence about the object and the circumstances surrounding its existence. As a result, if the authenticity of the information provided by the museum is compromised the identities of the creator or maker of cultural objects will remain muted. Therefore, it is unsurprising that the debate around the practice of objectifying, referencing and recontextualising cultural material by a state-funded museum has come under criticism in the museological discourse. Although the debate is not necessarily new, public museums must work towards developing a better classification system in an attempt to restore some heuristic dignity for unknown cultural object makers, and allow museum professionals to make informed decisions about their collections (Pearce, 1992:87).

Although there may be opposing opinions and views about the classification of the "unknown maker(s)" of cultural objects, the role of a publicly funded national museum is to recognise and research rare and unique cultural objects in their care. Museums should also implement the necessary protocols for culturally sensitive objects to better represent the diversity of their collections. By examining ISANG's art collection, this study concluded that classificatory activities within a museum setting are outweighed by the fundamental rules of identification nuances, particularly when a museum is unable to find an appropriate classification term for cultural objects and their makers. As a result, incomplete information has become a by-product of erasure over time, which can undermine the resilience of any historical account, especially when the life expectancy of museum information is centred on "maintaining and adding value to a trusted body of information for future use" (Poole, 2016:2).

This study showed that the author's or creator's biography diminished in his or her absence, and with the lack of information the responsibility to decode their work lay on the viewer. Although, the author's or creator's interpretation of their own work is only one of many possible interpretations (Barthes, 2001:3), the original understanding or intention of the work should be preserved. Therefore, cultural institutions must be mindful of how they preserve the artistic heritage of humankind, making cultural objects and their histories widely accessible while maintaining public confidence by following correct and rigorous research protocols.

Reference List

Abbott, D. 2008. What is digital curation? *Digital Curation Centre: Edinburgh*, UK. Available: http://www.dcc.ac.uk/resources/briefingpapers/introduction-curation/what-digital-curation. Accessed: October 2020.

Akinwale, A.A. 2012. *Digitisation of indigenous knowledge for natural resources management in Africa.* Paper presented at the 20th Anniversary Summit of the African Educational Research Network at North Carolina State University, Raleigh. Available:http://www.ncsu.edu/aern/TAS12.1/AERN2012Summit_Akinwale.pdf. Accessed May 2018.

Alford, R. 1988. Naming and identity: *A cross-cultural study of personal naming practice*, HRA Flex Books.

Andrews, R., Borg, E., Boyd Davis, S., Domingo, M. and England, J. (eds) 2012. *The Sage Handbook of Digital Dissertations and Theses* London: Sage: 544

Asogwa, B.E 2011. Digitization of archival collections in Africa for scholarly communication: issues, strategies, and challenges. *Journal of Library Philosophy and Practice*, University of Idaho Library.

Autry, R. 2017. *Desegregating The Past: the public life of memory in the United States and South Africa.* Columbia University Press, New York.

Barthes, R. 2001. The death of the author. *Contributions in Philosophy, 83*:3-8

Bell, J. A. 2017. A Bundle of Relations: Collections, Collecting, and Communities. *Annual Review of Anthropology 46 Journal Article.*

Benjamin, W. 1936. The work of art in the age of mechanical reproduction. *Visual Culture: Experiences in Visual Culture*: 144-137.

Bennett, T. 2013. The birth of the museum: *History, theory, and politics.* London and New York Routledge: 96-100.

Bernard, H.R. 2002. *Research Methods in Anthropology: Qualitative and quantitative methods. 3rd edition.* AltaMira Press, Walnut Creek, California.

Biebuyck, D.P. 1973. *Tradition and creativity in tribal art*, Berkeley, Los Angeles & London: University of California Press.

Bonoma, T.V., 1985. Case research in marketing: opportunities, problems, and a process. *Journal of marketing research*. 22(2):199-208.

Borowiecki, K.J., Forbes, N. and Fresa, A., 2016. *Cultural heritage in a changing world*. Springer Science and Business Media.

Bowen, G. A. 2009. Document analysis as a qualitative research method. *Qualitative Research*, 9 (2):27-40.

Bowker, G.C & Star, S.L., 1999. *Sorting things out: classification and its consequences*. Cambridge, Mass.: Mit Press, [Ca.

Britz, J. & Lor, P. 2004. A moral reflection on the digitization of Africa's documentary heritage. World Library and Information congress: 69th IFLA general conference. *IFLA Journal, 30 (3):* Sage Publications Sage CA: Thousand Oaks, CA 216-223.

Brink, H.I. 2003. *Fundamentals of research methodology for health care professionals*. Cape Town: Juta & Company.

Brown, B. 2001. Thing Theory, *Critical Inquiry*. 28(1):1-16

Bjerregaard, P.2006. The Materiality of Museum Politics: Moesgard Museum, University of Aarhus, Demark.

Cameron, F. 2007. "Beyond the Cult of the Replicant: Museums and Historical Digital Objects – Traditional Concerns, New Discourses." Theorizing Digital Cultural Heritage, A Critical Discourse. eds. Fiona Cameron and Sarah Kenderdine. Cambridge MA: MIT Press

Chowdhury, G & Ruthven, I. 2015. *Cultural heritage information*: Access and management. Facet Publishing.

Conway, P. 2010. Preservation in the age of google: Digitization, digital preservation, and dilemmas. *Journal Article the Library Quarterly*, The University of Chicago Press. Library Quarterly, 8 (1). Available http://www.editlib.org/p/106837 Accessed: May 2018

Cultural institution 2019, Wikipedia, viewed 31 May 2019. Available:
<https://www.wikiwand.com/en/Cultural_institution>. Accessed: May 2018

Davison, P. 1991. Material culture, context, and meaning: a critical investigation of museum
practice, with particular reference to the South African Museum. D. Phil book, University of
Cape Town.

Davison, P. 1990. Rethinking the practice of ethnography and cultural history in South African
museums. UCT. *African Studies,* 49(1):149-167.

Denzin, N.K. 2006. Analytic autoethnography, or déjà vu all over again. *Journal of contemporary
ethnography*, 35(4):419-428.

Denzin, N.K. 1978. The research act: *A theoretical introduction to sociological methods*. New York,
NY: McGraw-Hill.

Denzin, N.K. & Lincoln, Y.S. (eds.). 2011. *The Sage handbook of qualitative research*. 4th ed. Los
Angeles: Sage Publications.

Department of Arts and Culture 2010, *national policy on the digitisation of heritage resources final draft
for public review august 2010 v8 national department of arts and culture*. (n.d.). [online]
Available:
http://www.archivalplatform.org/images/resources/NATIONAL_POLICY_ON_DIGITISATION_V8.
Accessed: April 2018.

DeSilvey, C., 2006. Observed decay: Telling stories with mutable things. *Journal of material
culture*, 11(3): 318-338.

Deliss, C. 2015. *Collecting Life's Unknowns*. Online. Available:
http://www.internationaleonline.org/research/decolonising_practices/27collecting_lifes_unkno
wn Accessed: April 2018.

Dillman, D.A. 2001. Mail and Internet Surveys: *The Tailored Design Method. Brisbane*: Wiley.

Domínguez, R. V. 1988. 'On creating a material heritage', paper presented to the symposium 'The
Objects of Culture', annual meeting of the American Anthropological Association, Phoenix,
Ariz., [19 November]: 50-60.

Domínguez Rubio, F. 2014. Preserving the unpreservable: docile and unruly objects at MoMA. *Theory and Society*, [online] 43(6):617–645. Available at: https://link.springer.com/article/10.1007/s11186-014-9233-4 Accessed: 13 Jan. 2020.

Dudley, S. H 2009. Museum materialities: objects, sense and feeling, in Dudley, Sandra H. (ed), *Museum Materialities: Objects, Engagements, Interpretations*, Routledge, Taylor & Francis Group,2009. Imprint Routledge.

Erlandson, D.A, Harris, E.L., Skipper, B.L & Allen, S.D. 1993. Doing naturalistic inquiry: *a guide to methods*. London: Sage Publication.

Feger, H. 2001, Classification: *Conceptions in the social science*, Elsevier publication.

Fielding, R. T & Taylor, R. N. 2000. *Architectural Styles and the Design of Network-based Software Architectures*, book. University of California, Irvine. Available: http://dx.doi.org/10.2218/ijdc.v1i1.2 Accessed May 2018.

Finney, J. & Burnard, P. 2007. *Music Education with Digital Technology* (ed). New York Continuum International Publishing group.

Fleckner, J. 1991. "Dear Mary Jane": Some Reflections on Being an Archivist. *The American Archivist*: Winter 1991, 54(1): 8-13.

Foucault, M. 1970: The Order of Things, *An archaeology of the human sciences*. London and New York.

Fouché, C.B. and Schurink, W., 2011. Qualitative research designs. *Research at grassroots: For the social sciences and human service professions*, 4:307-327.

Douw, 2017. *AFRICAN ART AS PHILOSOPHY – Senghor, Bergson and the Idea of Negritude - Art Africa Magazine*. [online] Art Africa Magazine. Available: https://artafricamagazine.org/african-art-as-philosophy-2/ Accessed: March 2018.

Grobler, E 2006. Collections management practices at the transvaal museum, 1913 - 1964: anthropological, archaeological and historical. Doctor philosophy (museology). University of Pretoria.

Guiart, J. 1983. *Ethnographic museums: principles and problems*. Museum no 139; Published by the United Nations Educational, Scientific and Cultural Organization in Paris.

Guion, L.A. Diehl, D.C.& McDonald, D. 2011. Triangulation: establishing the validity of qualitative studies. Available: http://digitalcommons.unl.edu/libphilprac/421 Accessed: June 2019.

Hakim, C. 1987. Research Design: Strategies and Choices in the Design of Social Research, *Contemporary Social Research Series 13*. London: Allen and Unwin Hyman.

Hall, A.L. & Rist, R.C. 1999. Integrating multiple qualitative research methods (or avoiding the precariousness of a one-legged stool). *Psychology & Marketing*, 16(4):291-304.

Hall, S. 1980. Cultural studies and the Centre: some problematics and problems. *In Culture, Media, Language: Working Papers in Cultural Studies 1972-79*, edited by S. Hall. London and New York: Routledge.

Harris, V. 2002. Archival sliver: power, memory and archives in South Africa, *Archival Science no2* :63-86 available: http://wiredspace.wits.ac.za/bitsream/handle/10539/7871/HWS-166.pdf?sequence=1. Accessed: June 2019.

Hartley, J. 2004. Current findings from research on structured abstracts. *Journal of the Medical Library Association*, 92(3):368.

Harvey, R. 2005. Preserving digital Materials. Munich: Saur: K.G. Saur 2005. 246 pp., ISBN: 3-598-11686-1. *Journal of Documentation*, 62(6):765–768.

Hein, H.S. 2000. Museum typology, journal. *The Museum in Transition:* A Philosophical Perspective.

Henning, M. 2005. *Museums, media and cultural theory*. McGraw-Hill Education (UK).

International Organization for Standardization 2016, *International museum statistics*, ISO/DIS 18461 Available: https://www.iso.org/obp/ui/#iso:std:iso:18461:ed-1:v1:en Accessed: July 2019.

Howarth, F. 2018. *Decolonizing the Museum Mind*. [online] American Alliance of Museums. Available: https://www.aam-us.org/2018/10/08/decolonizing-the-museum-mind/ Accessed: 13 Jan 2020.

Kalusopa, T. & Zulu,T. 2009. Digital heritage material preservation in Botswana: Problems and prospects (28). University of Botswana, Collection Building.

Kelly, J. 2014. Colloquium: The ontological turn, where are we? Hau: *Journal of Ethnographic Theory*. University of Chicago, 4(1):1-5.

Kirshenblatt-Gimblett, B. 2004. *The Museum—A Refuge for Utopian Thought*. In J. Rüsen, M. Fehr & A. Ramsbrock (eds.). *Die Unruhe der Kultur: Potentiale des Utopischen*. Weilerswist.

Kreps, C.F. 2003. Liberating Culture: *Cross-Cultural Perspectives on Museums, Curation, and Heritage Preservation*. London: Routledge.

Kress, G. 2010. *A Social Semiotic Approach to Contemporary Communication*. London Routledge.

Kress, G. & van Leeuwen, T. 2001. Multimodal Discourse: *The modes and media of contemporary communication*. New York: Oxford University Press.

Lee, C., Tibbo, H., & Schaefer, J. 2007. "Defining What Digital Curators Do and What They Need to Know: The DigCCurr Project." *Proceedings of the 7th ACM/IEEE Joint Conference on Digital Libraries, Vancouver, British Columbia, Canada, June 18-23, 2007*, edited by Ron Larson, Edie Rasmussen, Shigeo Sugimoto, and Elaine Toms. New York: NY, ACM Press, pp.49-50.

Leedy, P.D. & Ormrod, J.E. 2005. *Practical Research: Planning and Design*. Prentice Hall, Upper Saddle River, NJ.

Macedo, Donaldo, L. Semali, and J. Kincheloe, 1999. "Decolonizing indigenous knowledge." What is indigenous knowledge*: Voices from the academy:* 134-176.

MacKenzie, J. 2009. South Africa: The South African Museum. In Museums and Empire: natural   history, human cultures and colonial identities. J. Mackenzie, Ed. Manchester: Manchester University Press: 4-10.

Manovich, L. 2001. *The language of new media*. Cambridge, MA: the MIT Press.

Marczyk, G., DeMatteo, D., & Festinger, D. 2005. *Essentials of research design and methodology*. Hoboken, NJ: John Wiley.

Mauss, M. 1969. *Oeuvres II Paris*: Eds de Minuit.

Mentz, M. 2012. Survey research. *In Doing social research: a global context*. C. Wagner, B. B. Kawulich & M. Garner, eds. London: McGraw Hill, pp.101.

Martin, M.R., 2010. *Legal issues in African art*. University of Lowa.

Moran-Ellis, J., Alexander, V.D., Cronin, A., Dickinson, M., Fielding, J., Sleney, J. and Thomas, H., 2006. Triangulation and integration: process, claims and implications. *Qualitative research*, 6(1), pp.45-59.

Morphy, H. 1999. Encoding the Dreaming – A theoretical framework for the analysis of representational processes in Australian Aboriginal art. *Australian Archaeology*, 49(1):13–22.

Nelson, M. 1997: *Former President Nelson Mandela Speech on Heritage Day, Robben Island Online 24 September 1997*. Available: http://www.mandela.gov.za/mandela_speeches/1997/970924_heritage.htm Accessed: February 2018.

Nicolaisen, W.F.J. 1976 *Words and Names*. Onoma (20)1: 142-163.

Nora, P. 1996. Realms of Memory: *Rethinking the French Past (Vol. I: Conflicts and Divisions)*. ed. New York: Columbia University Press.

Okon, E.E. 2013. *Distortion of Facts in Western Ethnographic Study of African Religion, Culture and Society*. International Journal of Asian Social Science.

Olsen, W., 2004. Triangulation in social research: *qualitative and quantitative methods can really be mixed. Developments in sociology,* (20):103-118.

Oguibe, O. 2004. *The Culture Games*. University of Minnesota Press.

Parekh, B.C. and Pieterse, J.N. eds. 1995. *The Decolonization of Imagination: Culture, Knowledge and Power*. Zed Books.

Parry, R. 2007. Recoding the museum: *Digital heritage and the technologies of change*. Routledge.

Paul, C. 2008. "Introduction." In C. Paul (ed.). *New Media in the White Cube and Beyond: Curatorial Models for Digital Art*. Leonardo Reviews Quarterly, (1). Oakland, CA: University of California Press.

Pearce, S. M. 1992. *Museum objects and collection: a cultural study*, Leicester University Press, London.

Poole, A.H. 2016. The conceptual landscape of digital curation. *Journal of Documentation*, 72(5): 961-986.

Poster, M. 2001. *What's the Matter with the Internet?* Minneapolis: University of Minnesota Press.

Proctor, N. 2010. Digital: Museum as platform, curator as champion, in the age of social media. *The Museum Journal,* Vol (53) 1, Blackwell Publishing Ltd Oxford, UK.

Routhier P, S., 2014. Digitization and digital preservation: A review of the literature. *School of Information Student Research Journal,* 4(1):4.

Semali, L.M. and Kincheloe, J.L., 2002. *What is indigenous knowledge? Voices from the academy.* Routledge.

Scerri, E. 2011. What is the nature of the periodic table as a classification system?

South African Heritage Resource Agency, 1999. *National Heritage Resource Act 25, Government Gazzete,* 28 April 1999, Vol 406 No. 19974, Notice No 506. Available: https://sahris.sahra.org.za/sites/default/files/website/articledocs/Sahra_Act25_1999.pdf Accessed: September 2020.

Stake, R.E. 1995. *The art Study Research: Perspectives in Practice.* London: Sage.

Stocking, G. W. (ed) 1985. *Objects and Others: Essays on Museums and Material Culture.* Wisconsin and London: University of Wisconsin Press.

Sullivan, G. (ed). 2010. *Art practice as research: Inquiry in visual arts.* Sage

Thibodeau, K. 2002. Overview of technological approaches to digital preservation and challenges in coming years. In the State of Digital Preservation: An International Perspective – Conference Proceedings. Washington, DC: Council on Library and Information Resources. Available: http://www.clir.org/pubs/reports/pub107/pub107.pdf. Accessed May 2018.

Tietze, A. 2017. A history of the Iziko South African National Gallery: *Reflections on art and national identity.* Juta and Company (Pty) Ltd.

Udofia, A .2016. Itibbesism African Ontology: A Prolegomenon to the Philosophy of Social Re-Engineering. *The 11th Biennial Collective Intentionality Conference paper.* Available: https://researchgate.net Accessed: May 2018.

University of Cambridge, 2019. *We ask the experts: why do we put things into museums?* Available:https://www.cam.ac.uk/research/discussion/we-ask-the-experts-why-do-we-put-things- into museums Accessed: 11 April 2019.

Van Beurden, S. 2015.Authentically African: *Arts and the transnational politics of Congolese culture*. Ohio University Press.

Van Malssen, K. 2012. Digital Video Preservation and Oral History. *The journal of Oral History in the Digital Age* (eds) D. Boyd, S. Cohen, B. Rakerd, and D. Rehberger. Washington, DC: Institute of Museum and Library Services. Available http://ohda. matrix. msu. edu/2012/06/digital-video-preservation-and-oral-history Accessed: June 2018.

Wanless, A. 2007. The Silence of Colonial Melancholy: *The Fourie Collection of Khoisan Ethnologica*. Vol 1. University of the Witwatersrand, Johannesburg.

Weyers, M. Strydom, H. and Huisamen, A. 2008. *Triangulation in social work research: the theory and examples of its practical application*. Social Work/Maatskaplike Werk, 44(2).

Williams, D. 1974. Icon and image: *A study of sacred and secular forms of African classical art*, Allen Lane press.

Yazan, B., 2015. Three approaches to case study methods in education: Yin, Merriam, and Stake. *The qualitative report*, 20(2):134-152.

Yin, R. K. 2009. *Case study research: design and methods*. 4th ed, Los Angeles: Sage Publications.

Appendices

Appendix A: Informed Consent

Subject: The digital classification of unknown makers: A case study of Iziko South African National Gallery.

Informed Consent

You have been invited to participate in a web-based online survey on the topic. The digital classification of *unknown* makers of cultural artefacts. A case study of Iziko South African National Gallery. The research project is being conducted by Sepadi Moruthane an MPhil Specialising in Digital Curatorship student (mrtsep001) with the Department of Knowledge and Information Stewardship (UCT).

By selecting "YES" below, you agree to the following.

PARTICIPATION

- I confirm that I have read and have understood the purpose of this research project and I have had the opportunity to ask questions about the project.
- I understand that my participation in this survey is voluntary and I may refuse to take part in the research or exit the survey at any time without penalty. In addition, should I not wish to answer any particular question or questions, I am free to decline.

CONFIDENTIALITY

- I am satisfied that my name will be kept anonymous and all the data collected will be kept confidential. My answers will be sent to a link at www.redcap.uct.ac.za where data will be stored in a protected electronic format. REDCap Survey Software web tool does not collect identifying information such as my name, email address, or IP address.
- I am comfortable to make a contribution to this research project and I am informed about how the results of this online survey will be handled.

CONTACT

- Any questions about the study or the procedures may be addressed to.

Student: Sepadi Moruthane   Supervisor: Richard Higgs

email: mrtsep001@myuct.ac.za   email: richard.higgs@uct.ac.za

Contact: 078 505 9969   Contact: 021 650 4546

By selecting "Yes" I give my consent to participate voluntarily in this research. I have been fully informed about the nature of this research and understand that responses are anonymous and confidential. I have not been offered any specific financial or other incentives to participate and I am aware that I may withdraw at any time.

- Yes
- No

reset

The survey will take approximately about 30 to 40 minutes to complete.

Thank you in advance for your participation.

Appendix B: Email Invitation for an Online Questionnaire

The Iziko Museums of South Africa

Subject: Invitation to participate in research: Digital classification of *unknown* makers.

My name is Sepadi Moruthane. I am conducting research at the University of Cape Town towards my MPhil specialising in Digital Curation (student number MRTSEP001). I am requesting your participation in an online survey of museum professionals from Iziko Museums of South Africa. My interest is in exploring curatorial questions with museum professionals who have intimate knowledge of Iziko permanent art collections. You have been selected based on your associated expertise.

My research topic is: *The Digital classification of unknown makers of cultural artefacts: A case study of Iziko South African National Gallery.* The purpose of this online questionnaire is to gather information regarding cultural artefacts created by the so-called *unknown maker*, and the influence that this has on how we identify and derive meaning from them. This research seeks to determine the nature of the technical and practical challenges that arise in dealing with the digital profiling of "unknown" makers in public art collections, by examining current practice in the Iziko museums around the capture, storage, and presentation of artefacts with *unknown* makers.

Your participation in this online survey is completely voluntary and all of your responses are anonymous. No personally identifiable information will be associated with your responses and if you wish to withdraw from the survey at any time you are free to do so.

The outcomes of this research may benefit the Iziko South Africa Museums by highlighting issues around how crucial information concerning *unknown* makers is catalogued according to museum practices or standards.

To participate in the survey, please click on the following link below:

REDCap survey hyperlink: https://trn-redcap.uct.ac.za/surveys/?s=8XXMNJPEC9

If you have any questions about this survey, or difficulty in accessing the link or completing the survey, please contact me or my supervisor:

Student:	Sepadi Moruthane	Supervisor:	Richard Higgs
email:	mrtsep001@myuct.ac.za	email:	richard.higgs@uct.ac.za
Contact:	078 505 9969	Contact:	021 650 4546

Thank you in advance for your participation.

Appendix C: Online Questions from the REDCap Hyperlink

CORE FUNCTION MUSEUM QUESTIONS

1 What is your occupation or designation at the museum?

Expand

2 Please briefly describe the work or activities you do at the
museum.

Expand

3 In your opinion, what is the importance of acquiring
artefacts/objects of historical significance by a state-funded
cultural institution like the Iziko Museums of South Africa?

Expand

4 To your knowledge, has the Iziko museum conducted an
audit of its holdings for digitisation purposes?

- Yes
- No
- Not sure

reset

ART COLLECTIONS MANAGEMENT QUESTIONS

5 To your knowledge, is there a curatorial manual or metadata
schema for staff members to adopt when classifying national
heritage assets?

- Yes
- No
- Not sure

reset

6 Please briefly describe the processes involved in profiling,
classifying and exhibiting Iziko's permanent art collections,
as you see them, as well as any strengths or weakness in
these processes.

Expand

7   Considering the complex histories involved in exhibiting
    exotic cultures and contested biographies, what systems are
    you aware of at Iziko to deal with the so-called unknown
    identities of ethnographic object makers?

Expand

8   What level of descriptive metadata vocabulary (keyword
    lists) do you think the museum should adopt to express
    incomplete or omitted information concerning an unknown
    maker/creator in the museum's official inventory?

Expand

9   Please briefly describe any challenges you encounter when
    documenting and cataloguing unidentified makers/creators
    of ethnographic objects.

Expand

DIGITAL PRESERVATION QUESTIONS

10 To your knowledge, does the Iziko Museums of South Africa
    have a digitisation policy?

    ○ Yes
    ○ No
    ○ Not sure

reset

Expand

11 Cultural institutions are transferring more of their documents
    and data into a digital formats. How, in your experience, does
    the Iziko museum provide context, provenance, and
    authorship information for digital objects, especially when
    the information is not made available?

Expand

79

12 Besides artefacts being a reflection of culture's past and
    present, what do you think is the museum's ethical stance
    and practice in classifying unknown makers of ethnographic
    objects without dehumanising them?

Expand

13 In your opinion, how does the museum represent cultural
    objects created by unknown ethnographic makers?

Expand

14 To what extend do you think Iziko museums' approach to
    cataloguing contributes to the erasure and omission of
    crucial information about artefacts from its official records?

Expand

15 Do you have any additional comments or information
    concerning the digital representation and classification of
    the so-called unknown maker that you think might be useful
    for this study?

Expand

Submit

Save & Return Later

Appendix D: Permission to Conduct Research from Iziko

Attention to: The Director of Iziko Art Collections and Digitization Department
Subject: Request to Conduct Research at ISANG.
Date: 22 October 2018

Dear: Sir / Madame

My name is Sepadi Moruthane (Student number: MRTSEP001) and I hope this e-mail finds you well. In pursuit of my Master's Programme Specializing in Digital Curation (Department of Knowledge and Information Stewardship /LIS5031W) at the University of the Cape Town, this letter hereby request permission to conduct a qualitative research study titled: The digital classification of *unknown* makers of cultural artefacts: A case study of Iziko South African National Gallery.

For this research to be coherent, a case study triangulation procedure also known as "methodological triangulation" will be adopted. I will require conducting a qualitative method of collecting data in the form of purposive sampling and performing an exhibition review reflecting on Iziko's permanent art collection (ISANG Art collection).

I hope that the information obtained from this research study will benefit Iziko Art Collections and Digitization Department in identifying different strategies, tactics, and methods of digital preservation. For further information you can contact my supervisor Richard Higgs email: richard.higgs@uct.ac.za or Andrew Lamprecht email: andrew.lamprecht@uct.ac.za and my contact details are: 0785059969 (mobile number) and e-mail sepadi2so@gmail.com

I look forward to hearing from you at your earliest convenient time.

Director's signature on behalf of the Iziko's Art Collections and Digitization Department:

Signature Removed

Signature : .... Date : 22/10/2018..............

Researcher signature: Signature Removed .... Date: 22/10/2018....

Yours Sincerely

Sepadi Moruthane.

DIGITIZATION POLICY

Version	1.0
Date of approval by Council	
Availability	Public and all staff
History	Version 1.0 1st draft completed 17 October 2014 by Hamish Robertson
	Version 1.0 2nd draft completed 21 October 2014
Responsible officer	Executive Director Core Functions
Contact	Iziko Museums of South Africa
	PO Box 61
	Cape Town
	8000
	Tel. 021 481 3800
	Email info@iziko.org.za

Contents

1. Introduction
2. Definitions
3. Guiding principles
4. Digitization strategy
5. Digital preservation
6. Access

DIGITIZATION POLICY

1.   INTRODUCTION

Iziko Museums of South Africa (Iziko) has large, diverse collections that are used to benefit society through research, expert services, education, exhibitions, tourism, publications and online platforms. Digitization and the associated processes of digital preservation and digital access have become critical to the strategy for promoting both the preservation of these collections and the benefit that the broad public can derive from them.

The diversity of Iziko's collections reflects the history of South Africa (and beyond) from rocks laid down 3200 million years ago containing microscopic vestiges of early life, to fossils showing the origin of mammals 225 million years ago, to human origins in the past 4 million years, to early symbolic human expression in the form of the 75 000 year-old engraved ochre from the southern Cape, to 1500 year-old iron-age ceramics from Mpumalanga, to engraved postal stones of 16th and 17th European ships coming round the Cape, to colonial (AD 1652 plus) buildings and artifacts reflecting the Dutch and British occupations of the Cape, to art and artifacts of the 20th Century reflecting the tumultuous history of that century, to the symbols, art and artifacts representing the change to a democratic South Africa in 1994 and reflecting new forms of creativity.

The Natural History collections include over 269 000 catalogued fossils and rocks representing the history of life on earth, and over 422 000 catalogued zoological collection objects, reflecting the rich biodiversity of South Africa and beyond. Including uncatalogued collection objects and excluding the library, images and archives, there are about 1.86 million collection objects in Natural History. The palaeontological collections include the world renowned tetrapods from the South African Karoo basin including rare fossils representing the most ancient ancestors of mammals, turtles and dinosaurs (300-200 million years ago) as well as thousands of fossils from Langebaanweg, regarded as the richest terrestrial fossil occurrence of Early Pliocene age (5 million years ago) in the world. The zoological collections are the largest in South Africa with particular strengths in: Hymenoptera (ants, bees and wasps), terrestrial vertebrate osteology, marine invertebrates, marine mammals, and fish. These biological collections constitute an essential national scientific facility, providing foundational services to research, agriculture, fisheries, medicine, and conservation, besides their value for educational purposes.

The Social History collections total about 243 000 catalogued collection objects. The archaeology collections include pre-colonial and historical archaeology mainly from coastal areas round South Africa; there is also the Human Remains collection that contains approximately 1400 individuals. Within this collection are about 150 unethically collected individuals that need to be de-accessioned (see Human Remains Policy). The material culture collections include furniture and household objects, ceramics, beadwork, jewellery, personal adornment and personal objects, textiles and costume, basketry, glass, metalware, coins and other means of exchange, stamps, weapons and armour, musical instruments, religious artefacts, memorabilia, tools and equipment, scientific instruments, transport, ship models and maritime artefacts, historical oil paintings, watercolours, prints and drawings, paper-based objects, and oral history recordings.

The Art collections include about 9850 catalogued items, including: painting and sculpture; prints and drawings; photography and new media; and African art.

Additional to the above collections are the photographic and document collections making up the Iziko Archive – the number of these items is uncertain as they still need to be properly

2

sorted and organized but it comes to well over 350 000 items. Also additional, are the library collections, which include unique, archival items that need to be digitized.

From the above summary, it is clear that Iziko's collections are an amazingly rich record of our world and its past that can be leveraged through digitization to benefit society on a broad front. In addition to the benefits digitization will bring to research and education, it is also important in terms of meeting the new accounting standards of GRAP103 and for general management of these collections.

Digitization of Iziko's collections started as far back as 1990, with capturing of metadata from the natural history collections, with Art and Social History subsequently joining in. Of all the catalogued collection objects in Iziko (944 000, excluding libraries), the metadata is digitized for about 73% of Natural History items, 15% of Social History items and about 97% of Art items. Imaging of these objects has been fragmentary and *ad hoc* with little integration with the metadata databases.

Selected digitized information is accessible on the internet: some Natural History biodiversity metadata has been made accessible on the GBIF and OBIS websites; Africa Media Online host selected art images, and the SARADA site hosts Iziko rock art information and images. However, for the most part, Iziko's digitized data is currently inaccessible to a broad audience. There are also many objects in Iziko's collections that require sorting, documentation and accessioning before they can be digitized.

While digitization is an important priority for Iziko, it is being undertaken in the absence of a digital preservation strategy, which poses significant risks. Data on servers are backed up but there are large bodies of data that are not on the servers and which are backed up in an *ad hoc* manner. Digital preservation amounts to more than just backing up of data – data migration to new hardware and software platforms is essential, and data in the system need to be properly contextualised and provenanced with appropriate metadata. The Open Archival Information Systems (OAIS) standard (ISO 14721:2012) is now the main international standard for digital preservation. The recent development of open source, free, Archivematica software (funded by a number of agencies, including UNESCO Memory of the World; see https://www.archivematica.org/wiki/Main_Page) makes it much easier to implement this standard but to do so effectively requires significant investment in human resources.

This first version of Iziko's Digitization Policy is a first step towards a mature policy that is underpinned by procedures, a digitization and digital preservation strategy, and an organisational structure that enables appropriate focus on the creation, preservation and use of Iziko's digital assets. Thus, this policy should be seen as preliminary and will be revised again within the next two years.

1.1. Purpose

1.1.1. To provide a policy framework on which to build and guide Iziko's digitization strategy.

1.1.2. To provide principles for best practice in digitization, digital preservation, and digital access.

1.1.3. To clarify the legal framework for digitization to ensure that legal obligations are met.

3

1.2. Scope

1.2.1. This policy applies to digitized items, born digital items, and physical items that need to be digitized. The latter physical items include all items that have been accessioned into Iziko collections with identifying catalogue numbers (but see 1.2.2 below). These include accessioned collection objects and archival items (documents, photographs, tape recordings and videos).

1.2.2. Digitization in terms of photography and scanning does not include Unethically Collected Human Remains, which form a closed collection, not for public study, available only for repatriation.

1.2.3. This policy applies to the process of digitization as well as digital preservation and digital access. In the absence of an Archive Policy and an Intellectual Property Policy, it also expresses some important principles in regard to archiving and copyright that pertain to digitization.

1.3. Legal framework

1.3.1. **Constitution of the Republic of South Africa, Act 108 of 1996, as amended**. Section 32(1) in the Bill of Rights states: "Everyone has the right of access to … any information held by the state".

1.3.2. **Promotion of Access to Information Act 2 of 2000**. Gives effect to the constitutional right of access to any information held by the State, subject to justifiable limitations, including, but not limited to, limitations aimed at the reasonable protection of privacy, commercial confidentiality and effective, efficient and good governance (Section 9 (i)). Amongst other things, access to information can be turned down if it amounts to an infringement of copyright not owned by the public body concerned (Section 29 (4) (c)), or if disclosure will prejudice or impair the security of property (Section 38 (b) (i)), or if disclosure will seriously disadvantage research being undertaken (Section 43). Right of access needs to be swift, inexpensive and as effortless as reasonably possible (Section 9 (d)). This Act is aimed at promoting transparency, accountability and effective governance of all public and private bodies, and empowering and educating everyone (Section 9 (e)).

1.3.3. **Cultural Institutions Act, 1998 (Act No. 119 of 1998)**. Section 8 (1) (a) states that one of the functions of a Council of a Declared Cultural Institution is "to receive, hold, preserve and safeguard all specimens, collections or other movable property placed under its care and management…". Digitization is an important part of the strategy for preservation of these items. This Act is silent on promoting the educational value of collections.

1.3.4. **National Heritage Resources Act, 1999 (Act 25 of 1999)**. Section 32 (7) states that "SAHRA [the South African Heritage Resources Agency] must maintain a register of heritage objects in which all objects, collections of objects and types of objects which have been declared heritage objects must be listed".

Section 39 (1) states that "…SAHRA must compile and maintain an inventory of the national estate, which must be in the form of a data base of information on heritage resources which it considers worthy of conservation".

Government Notice no. 1512 (6 December 2002) lists the types of heritage objects deemed to be protected in terms of the National Heritage Resources Act. A high proportion of items in Iziko's collections are covered by this list, including all archaeological, palaeontological specimens; rare geological specimens; meteorites; ethnographic objects; objects relating to South African history; art that has been in South Africa for more than 50 years; coins and medals that have been in South Africa for more than 100 years; manuscripts, books, documents, publications, photographs, sound recordings that have been in South Africa for

4

more than 50 years; antiquities, furniture and other cultural objects that are older than 100 years; and zoological, botanical and geological specimens that have been in South Africa for more than 100 years.

1.3.5. **National Environmental Management: Biodiversity Act No. 10 of 2004.** Section 49 on monitoring of biodiversity states that "The Minister must …designate monitoring mechanisms and set indicators to determine … the conservation status of various components of South Africa's biodiversity …The Minister may require any person, organization or organ of state involved in [monitoring] to report regularly to the Minister on the results of such monitoring…". Iziko's zoological collections make a significant contribution to the monitoring of South African biodiversity, with digital information provided to the South African Biodiversity Information Facility (SABIF; managed by SANBI), which in turn provides information to the Global Biodiversity Information Facility (GBIF).

1.3.6. **Accounting Standards Board: Standard of Generally Recognised Accounting Practice – Heritage Assets (GRAP 103).** The Accounting Standards Board is required in terms of the Public Finance Management Act No. 1 of 1999 to determine Standards of Generally Recognised Accounting Practice (GRAP). The GRAP 103 Standard specifies that government entities need to list and value their heritage assets and include heritage assets in the financial statements. There is no specification of digitization but in view of the huge number of heritage assets held by museums like Iziko, it is essential that digital means are used to compile and update lists of heritage assets. Greater clarity is needed on whether the digital objects themselves need to be accounted for under GRAP 103.

1.4. Spirit

This policy has been developed in the spirit of:

1.4.1. enabling digital access to Iziko's collections for research, education, artistic and management purposes;

1.4.2. contributing data from Iziko's collections to broad-scale research and monitoring initiatives;

1.4.3. preserving Iziko collections by minimising handling of objects and preserving digital copies of objects;

1.4.4. ensuring that there is an ethical basis to digitization;

1.4.5. ensuring that digitization and digital preservation is undertaken according to international norms and standards;

1.4.6. compliance with GRAP 103 standards;

1.4.7. maximizing the value of Iziko's collections through integration and connection of data entities from various sources such as collection objects, photographs and archives;

1.4.8. enabling and promoting innovative, creative, cutting edge approaches to digitization and use of digital assets; and

1.4.9. providing a framework for a digitization strategy that is dynamic and able to adapt to, and embrace, new developments.

5

2. DEFINITIONS

2.1. **Born digital.** Information that was in digital format from the start such as photographs taken with a digital camera.

2.2. **Commercial use.** In this context this term applies to the use of digital objects for making money, e.g. the use of a photograph in a book that is sold for profit.

2.3. **Creative work.** A tangible object (analogue or digital) that is the result of a creative process. It might be a work of art (painting, drawing, sculpture), a photograph, a video, music, a design, or literature.

2.4. **Iziko Digital Repository.** The integrated digital system within which Iziko's digital objects are stored.

2.5. **Digital assets.** All digitized objects designated for long-term preservation.

2.6. **Digital object.** A defined item within a digital system, most typically a file (e.g. image file, pdf file).

2.7. **Digital preservation.** Digital preservation combines policies, strategies and actions to ensure access to digital content over time by ensuring that the structure, provenance and meaning of the digital information is explicit and understandable over time, and overcoming the problems of media failure and technological change.

2.8. **Digitization.** Digitization is the process of converting information into computer readable, digital format. Examples include: data entry on to computer, digital photography and scanning of documents.

2.9. **GRAP 103.** See under 1.3.6

2.10. **Intellectual property.** Legally recognized exclusive rights to creative works. For instance, an artist will typically sell a work but retain intellectual property rights over copying the work for other uses.

2.11. **OAIS.** Open Archival Information System, which is the main international standard (ISO 14721:2012) for digital preservation. It was developed by The Consultative Committee for Space Data Systems (CCSDS) from which a free version can be obtained (public.ccsds.org/publications/archive/650x0m2.pdf).

2.12. **Public domain.** Creative works that can be freely accessed and used by the general public because their intellectual property rights have expired or have been forfeited.

3. GUIDING PRINCIPLES

3.1. Digitization is an act of preservation in that it provides a digital copy of the original object, and hence is able to provide valuable information on that object should it later deteriorate or be destroyed. It also means that handling of the original object is reduced.

3.2. Digital copies are not replacements for original heritage objects and as such there must be continued care of the original objects, in compliance with Iziko's Collections Policy.

3.3. All catalogued objects in Iziko's collections should be digitized; digitization should usually include a digital representation of the object (e.g. digital photograph, sound recording, or video) and always include digital metadata fully describing the object, its context and provenance.

3.4. The pace of digitization is funding dependent. Digitization is time-consuming and in order to achieve full digitization of Iziko's collections, extensive external funding is required.

6

3.5. A skilled cross-departmental team, including representatives from collections and IT, is required to achieve digitization and ensure ongoing digital preservation.

3.6. Digitization provides the opportunity to improve access to Iziko collections and Iziko's digitization strategy will be focused on providing free access to information on its collections, provided in an attractive and informative manner.

3.7. In the absence of an Iziko Archive and Records Management Policy, born digital information that is potentially archival in nature, whether it be documents, spreadsheets, databases, emails or images, should be retained and digitally preserved to similar standards as catalogued digital objects, until such time that it can be properly processed and filtered within the framework of a policy.

3.8. Quality control is an essential component of the digitization workflow. There need to be clear quality standards developed that ensure accuracy and consistency, and these need to be enforced through appropriate training of staff and checking of data entered. The Iziko Digital Repository also needs to be subject to external quality audits to ensure that it meets international standards.

3.9. Information on the copyright status of each digital object will be recorded and used to control the correct use of that object.

3.10. A digital object without accompanying copyright information, that is not in the public domain, will be used for internal (Iziko staff) purposes only.

4. DIGITIZATION STRATEGY

4.1. Iziko will develop a Digitization Strategy that includes the following components.

4.1.1. An analysis of each collection in Iziko (objects, archives, images and other media), including assessment of:

- size
- composition
- condition for digitization
- rarity value
- conservation status (including vulnerability of collection to handling)
- intellectual property status (copyright issues)
- frequency of usage of collection (research visitors, loans, exhibitions)
- intellectual value
- digitization status
- metadata standards applicable
- digital access strategy (who will benefit from digitization and how)
- recommended software
- imaging/scanning strategy (equipment, resolution, number and size of files per object)
- human resources requirements for digitization

7

4.1.2.   A roll-out plan for digitization that prioritizes collections for digitization in terms of preservation and access.

4.1.3.   A digital preservation plan.

4.1.4.   A strategy for optimizing access to Iziko digital resources (stakeholders and beneficiaries, marketing).

4.1.5.   A funding model and fundraising strategy that takes into account Iziko's requirement to retain ownership and copyright.

4.1.6.   A human resources strategy to form a cross-departmental team, including required positions, and a skills development strategy.

4.1.7.   A Risk Management Plan including reputation risk.

4.1.8.   An infrastructure strategy (equipment, servers, outsourcing considerations including cloud storage, imaging studios).

4.2.   The Digitization Strategy will be incorporated within Iziko's Strategic Plan and Annual Performance Plans.

4.3.   Iziko will make every effort to coordinate its digitization strategy with international and national initiatives, through its representation in relevant forums and meetings.

5.   DIGITAL PRESERVATION

5.1.   Iziko will follow the Open Archival Information Systems (OAIS) standard (ISO 14721:2012) for preservation of its digital assets.

5.2.   Procedures for preservation of Iziko's digital assets will be developed according to OAIS standards, and implemented.

5.3.   Progress in achieving full compliance with OAIS standards will be monitored internally and audited externally on a regular basis (at least once every three years).

5.4.   Metadata standards will be implemented in a manner that ensures interoperability and sharing of digital resources.

6.   ACCESS

6.1.   Iziko will develop its own internet portal for providing information from its digital repository.

6.2.   Information will be provided in attractive manner that meets the needs of researchers, artists, educators, students, learners, and the interested public. Tools will be provided to search and present the information in useful and engaging ways.

6.3.   All digitization will be undertaken with the intention of making the materials freely accessible on the internet for non-commercial, educational, personal and fair use, except where there are limitations on use as specified under 6.5.

6.4.   Commercial use of Iziko-copyrighted digitized materials, other than metadata, is subject to application and charges.

6.5.   Information will be subject to controlled access where:

6.5.1.   it would jeopardize the security of the physical object (e.g. data on where it is stored). Objects must be securely housed before digital information about them is provided online;

8

6.5.2.   divulging the place where the object was collected would increase the vulnerability of other similar objects. For instance, providing the precise location of a rare type of fossil or endangered species, could expose them to further collecting by unscrupulous agents;

6.5.3.   copyright restrictions apply; and

6.5.4.   there are ethical issues relating to infringement of human rights and sensibilities. Until such time that there is an Iziko Ethics Policy and Ethics Committee, decisions on ethical control will be taken by the CEO or someone so delegated.

6.6.   Iziko will ensure that relevant information from its databases is accessible on public service web platforms that share similar objectives, subject to a Memorandum of Agreement with the relevant controlling body. Important web platforms include SAHRIS (managed by SAHRA), SA Biodiversity Information Facility (SABIF) and other SANBI managed sites, Global Biodiversity Information Facility (GBIF), Ocean Biogeographic Information System (OBIS), palaeontological databases managed by the Centre of Excellence for the Palaeosciences (Wits University), and the SA Rock Art Digital Archive (SARADA).

9

an agency of the
Department of Arts and Culture

TERMS OF REFERENCE

Art Acquisitions Committee

Background

The inclusion of an artwork in Iziko's art collections should be an indication that it has artistic merit and is worthy of inclusion in this premier, national, public art repository. Accepting or rejecting a work is inevitably a subjective exercise and any one person can be influenced by a range of factors, some more relevant than others. The Art Acquisitions Committee provides a way of gathering together representatives who are qualified to assess the merits of artworks and whose opinions can be tested against one another. The South African National Gallery has had an Art Acquisitions Committee for most of its existence, and under the pre-Iziko dispensation it was a sub-committee chaired by an external, art-qualified Trustee that reported directly to the SA National Gallery's Board of Trustees.

The policy on acquisitions into the Iziko collections is laid down in the Iziko Art Collections Policy. The Art Acquisitions Committee is not mentioned in this policy but is a critical element in ensuring due diligence, especially in view of the fact that artworks of great cultural, historical and commercial value are often considered.

Relevant clauses pertaining to the Iziko Art collections from the policy are provided below. The acronym 'ACD' refers to the Art Collections Department, which is technically no longer in existence – the acquisitions function is now under the aegis of the new Research and Exhibitions Department, which works in close liaison with the new Collections and Digitisation Department.

4.1 Aim and scope

The development of collections is fundamental to the vitality of Iziko. Collecting strategies of the individual departments are contained in separate documents that are regularly reviewed. Collection development will be prioritised in accordance with the strategic goals of Iziko, and in relation to the capacity of Iziko to house and manage new additions to the collections

4.1.3 The ACD builds a national collection that reflects the history of South African art, as well as the range of contemporary visual art production; one that reveals the diverse cultural roots of our art. As a national art museum, Iziko will acquire mainly South African art and where budget permits continental and international works of art.

4.2.1 The approval procedure for acquisitions is as follows:

4.2.1.1 Proposed acquisitions (purchases and donations) are discussed and selected by the individual department based on motivations regarding their significance, affordability, the department's collection strategy, as well as practical issues such as storage requirements and future costs of safekeeping and preservation.

4.2.1.2 Approval for donations and for purchases under R5000 is delegated to the Director of Exhibitions and Research who can authorize payment. The acquisitions are noted and approved by the Core Functions Management Committee and the Executive Director:Core Functions.

4.2.1.3 Recommendations for purchases and donations valued above R5000 but below R20 000 are made by the Director of Exhibitions and Research to the Core Functions Management Committee. Final approval is delegated to the Executive Director: Core Functions who can authorize payment. The acquisitions are noted in the reports of the Corporate Governance and Compliance Committee.

4.2.1.4 Recommendations for purchases and donations valued above R20 000 but below R100 000 are made by the Director of Director of Exhibitions and Research to the Core Functions Management Committee and the Executive Director: Core Functions. If supported by the Executive Director: Core Functions, these are taken forward to the Corporate Governance and Compliance Committee for approval. The acquisitions are then submitted to the Iziko Chief Executive Officer for final ratification, at which point payment can be made.

4.2.1.5 Recommendations for purchases and donations valued above R100 000 are made by the Director of Director of Exhibitions and Research to the Core Functions Management Committee and the Executive Director: Core Functions. If supported by the Executive Director: Core Functions these are taken forward to the Corporate Governance and Compliance Committee for approval, where the CEO gives the final authoritative recommendation, and then to the Council for final ratification, at which point payment can be made.

4.2.1.6 The CEO may withdraw the above delegations as and when deemed necessary.

4.2.1.9 Where material is offered to Iziko that would be more appropriate in another museum, donors will be referred to the other institution.

4.6 Study Collection

The Study Collection in the ACD is accessioned as part of the permanent collection but distinguished by an addition of a suffix 'S'. These are objects which might not be considered finished works of art, but which relate to the creation of a specific work in the collection or to processes used in the work of an artist in the collection. Preparatory sketches could be considered part of the Study Collection or alternatively as independent works of art in themselves. For instance, a cancelled printmaking matrix and preliminary section of a casting or a mould from a sculpture also constitute Study Collection objects. In the past, education collections of African art have also been accessioned as part of the Study Collection.

4.9 Donations

4.9.1 Donations must conform to the collecting priorities of Iziko, and will be accepted subject to agreed conditions.

4.9.2 The ownership of items donated must be established before material is accepted.

4.9.3 Donated material must be accompanied by full documentation.

4.9.4 Iziko will record and adhere to subsisting and future intellectual property rights attached to objects acquired.

4.9.5 Donated or bequeathed collections are not normally accepted if there are conditions attached.

4.9.6 Some donation agreements may be preceded with a request for the donor to assist in collection management and curatorial costs.

4.9.7 Proposed donations of material from outside South Africa will be accepted if they are not listed as being protected by legislation in their country of origin and if they do not violate the ethical requirements of this policy. The material will not be accepted if there is any possibility of a request for repatriation.

4.9.8 All donations and bequests of collections become part of the Iziko permanent collection and both parties, or their representatives, sign an agreement to this effect.

4.10 Bequests

The same conditions apply as for Donations. Copies of relevant legal documents must be lodged with the collections department.

4.11 Purchases

4.11.1 Purchases are made by the collections departments in accordance with their respective collecting strategies. As with donations, due diligence will be paid to clarifying legal ownership of material offered for purchase and Iziko will not knowingly acquire any material with a doubtful provenance.

4.11.2 Objects will not be bought for the collection unless funding has first been secured and the purchase price represents good and fair value for the money.

4.11.3 Iziko will record and adhere to subsisting and future intellectual property rights attached to the objects acquired.

1. **Objectives and Responsibilities**

1.1. To suggest works for purchase, to be considered by the Committee.

1.2. To consider the merits of works that have been offered to Iziko by donation or bequest.

1.3. To identify potential ethical issues in the acquisition of works.

1.4. To make recommendations for the acquisition of works.

2. **Membership**

2.1. Nominations for new external members will be called for from the responsible Iziko art curators by the Iziko Core Functions department.

2.2. The Acquisitions Committee will be a standing committee and at the end of the term of a member (or their departure for some other reason), the Chairperson will call for nominations for a replacement. Nominations will be reviewed by the Iziko art curators and they will make recommendations to the Core Functions Committee for approval and include the full list of nominations.

2.3. Membership of this committee is subject to members holding appropriate qualifications in Fine Art, Art History and Theory, Literary Studies, Performance, Visual/Cultural Studies or at least a record of respected production and/or publications germane to the visual arts.

2.4. A serving member may not be affiliated or related to any commercial entities that might financially benefit or otherwise from their participation.

2.5. The external representatives on the Acquisitions committee will consist of no more than six external members, including a representative of the Friends of the SA National Gallery. In addition, all Iziko art curators, the Iziko Collections Manager for Art collections, the Art Collections Registrar (or the staff member fulfilling this function) and the Iziko Senior Art Educator will be represented on the committee.

2.6. **Term of Office**

2.6.1. The term of each external member will be five years, starting from when they have accepted nomination. The member will be informed in writing and should acknowledge acceptance in writing (email will do).

2.6.2. An external committee member may only serve one term on the Acquisitions Committee.

2.6.3. An external committee member may stand down from the committee before their five years is complete. In such cases, they should inform the Chair of their decision in writing.

3. **Chairperson and Secretariat**

3.1. The Chair of the Committee will be one of the art curators and will be appointed by Iziko on a rotating basis.

4. **Quorum**

4.1. At least 50% plus one of the Committee must be present in order to constitute a quorum.

4.2. Members must endeavour to be present in order to contribute to the process.

5. **Meeting Frequency**

5.1. Meetings will be called by the Chairperson and

5.2. The committee must meet at least three times every financial year (1 April to 31 March).

5.3. Under exceptional circumstances, in particular where there is urgency in acquiring a work that has become available, Committee approval for acquisition of works may also be obtained from committee members via email, provided there is consensus. Where there is not consensus, the proposed acquisition should be presented at the next meeting for discussion, if it is still available. The Chairperson must keep records of email approvals and include them in the next meeting's minutes where a record should be made in the minutes of approvals that have taken place via email since the previous meeting. At least 75% of the committee must respond to the email request for the approval to be valid.

6. **Minutes and Reporting Protocol**

   6.1. In preparation for the meeting, members will be supplied timeously with details of the proposed works, Minutes of the previous meeting, and the Agenda.

   6.2. Minutes must be taken of meetings and an attendance register completed.

7. **Approval of works**

   7.1. Recommendations for works to be accepted into the collection will usually be based on consensus by the committee. Where there is a difference of opinion and failure to reach consensus, a work may still be recommended if more than 50% of the members support its acquisition. A record should be kept in the minutes of the issues involved.

   7.2. Acquisition recommendations by the Art Acquisitions Committee will be submitted to the Director Research and Exhibitions for presentation at the Core Functions Committee. The Chair of the Art Acquisitions Committee may be invited to the Core Functions Committee to make a presentation on the recommendations should this be necessary.

   7.3. Art acquisitions recommended by the Art Acquisitions Committee and approved by the Core Functions Committee will be presented to Iziko's Exco and Council for approval, in accordance with approved policy (see policy extracts under 'background', above).

8. **General**

   8.1. The Committee can request a committee member to recuse themselves on a particular matter if it is deemed that their participation or behaviour is not constructive to the committee mandate.

   8.2. There is no financial remuneration for participation on the Committee.

   8.3. Committee members are entitled to free entrance to the museums in Iziko Museums of South Africa for the duration of their tenure.

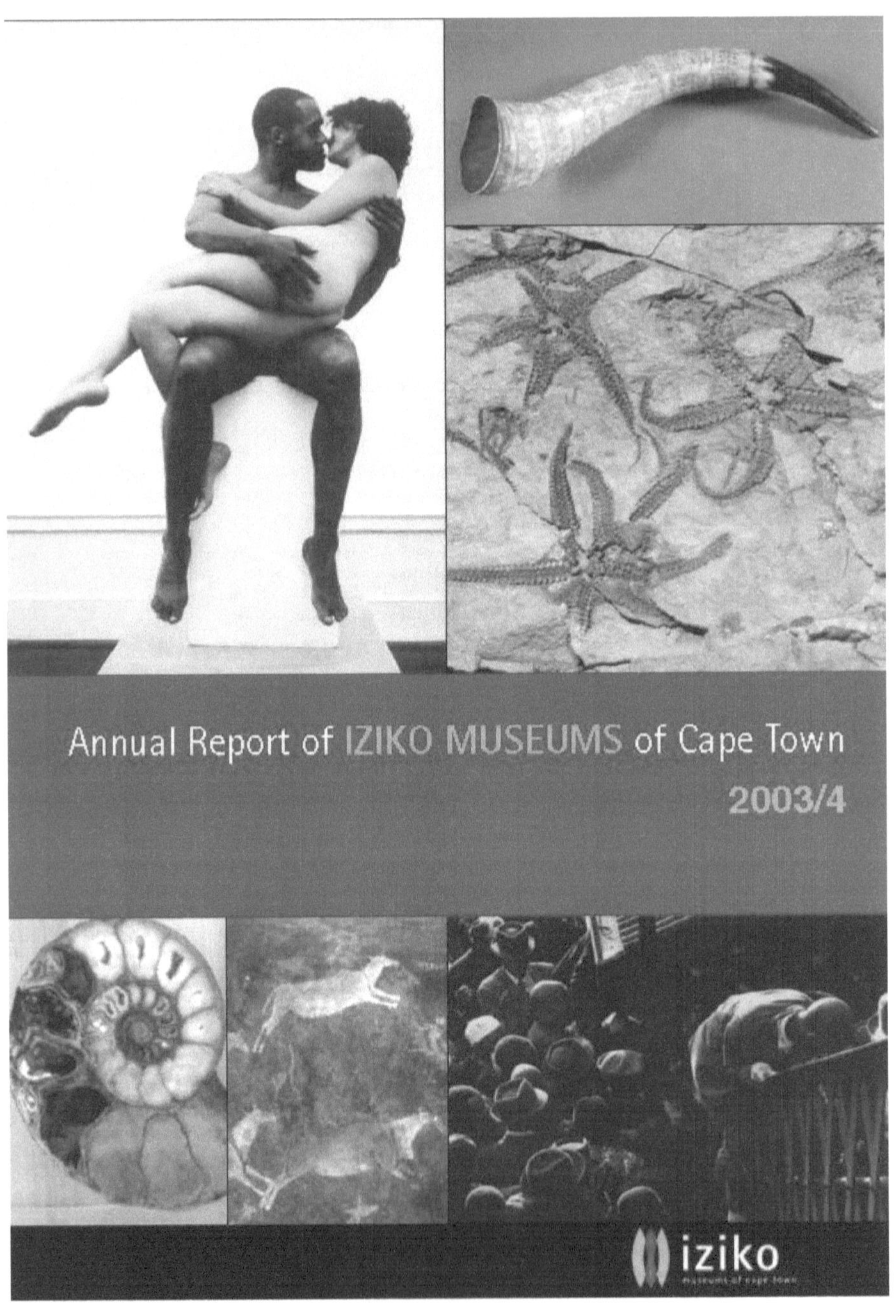
Annual Report of IZIKO MUSEUMS of Cape Town
2003/4
iziko
museums of cape town

Sorbaan, Mecca, Saudi Arabia, 1983.

Silver presentation keys and trowels belonging to Mr. Harry Gordon Lawrence (1901-1973), member of the South African Parliament from 1929-1961.

19th century furniture from the Pellemans bequest.

Record 150 Flooring Clamps of the screw type.

ART COLLECTIONS DIVISION

Work purchased from a transformation fund grant of R700 000 that was made available by the Department of Arts and Culture

Repatriation

Cow horn engraved with scenes of the Anglo-Zulu War, circa 1879, North Nguni, South-East Africa, R70 184,00, from Michael Stevenson Contemporary

Stick with a figure of an African man with a headring, late 19th century, SE Africa, R162 000,00, from Michael Stevenson Contemporary

Stick with a baboon figure, late 19th century, R37 737,00, from Michael Stevenson Contemporary

Albert Adams *Celebration* (2002), oil on canvas, R94 281,00, from the artist in London

Previously disadvantaged artists

Sipho Ndlovu *Organic ploughing* (2003), oil on canvas, R16 000,00, from the artist

Mgcineni Pro Sobopha *Blanket series* (2000), branding on textile, 3 at R8 000,00 each, R24 000,00, from the artist

Thando Mama *(un)hea(r)d* (2002), DVD, R6 000,00 and

We are Afraid (2003), R6 000,00, from the artist

Robin Rhode *He Got Game* (2001), DVD, R21 587,00, from the artist

Tracey Rose *The Kiss* (2001), lambda print, R23 190,00, from the Goodman Gallery

Usha Seejarim *The Opposite of Illustration 1* (1999), DVD, R5 000,00 and

Sequence City (2002), griplocks and cotton on silk sari, R17 000,00, from the artist

Moshekwa Langa *Where do I begin?* (2001), video, R25 850,00, from the Goodman Gallery

Colbert Mashile *Tsa Ka Mafuri (Lurking Behind)* (2003), gouache on paper, R17 833,00, from the NSA Gallery, Durban

The Egazini Battle of Grahamstown (2000), portfolio of 28 prints, R25 536,00, from Dominique Thorburn

Thembinkosi Goniwe *Untitled*, from *Returning the Gaze* (2000), pigment ink on cotton

xiii

Appendix I: Mr. Max Leipold Masks Bequest

BACKGROUND

Iziko Museums of South Africa was recently offered a bequest of a number of items for its collections of African art by Mr Max Leipold of Hermanus. Mr Leipold was referred to Iziko Museums by the then-Director of Zeitz MOCAA because the collection of pre-21st century items falls outside of their institutional mandate.

Mr Hayden Proud and Ms Carol Kaufmann, former Iziko Curator of African art, visited Mr Leipold in Hermanus to assess his intended bequest. The collection was fully documented and was put together in the 1940s and 50s by the Mr Leipold's father, the late Benno Leipold. Carol Kaufmann was impressed by the quality of the objects and their provenance. She strongly recommended the acceptance of the intended bequest, and this was also approved by the Iziko Art Collections Acquisitions Committee. Mr Leipold accordingly instructed his lawyer to insert this bequest to Iziko Museums in his last will and testament.

More recently, Mr Leipold contacted us again with a fresh proposal that he donate a part of the intended bequest (this being his collection of ten African masks) to Iziko Museums with immediate effect. The collection team and I visited Mr Leipold in Hermanus to collect these ten masks, two of which required isolation and treatment for insect activity. Mr Leipold expressed the wish that he and his wife come to Iziko Museums in the later part of June to formally present the collection to us. Since the Acquisitions Committee has already approved these items, it would be appreciated if Iziko Exco/Core Functions could formally approve the acceptance of these acquisitions. Carol Kaufmann has been consulted, and the Art Collections exhibitions committee has also approved that these items be inserted into the existing *Hidden Treasures* exhibition now on display in Rooms 10 and 11 of the Iziko SA National Gallery.

MOTIVATION

The existing collection of African art, as presently held by Iziko Art Collections, has only one example of an African mask which was purchased in the 1960s when Professor Bruce Arnott was the Assistant Director under Professor Matthys Bokhorst. The Leipold collection of ten masks will substantially increase the variety and profile of the African mask-form in our collection. It must be noted that the mask tradition in Africa does not extend further south than the Zambesi River, and that, as a consequence, given geographical and political issues in the past, our own collections of material from West and Central Africa have until recently been relatively thin. Our holdings in the latter areas, especially of West African material, were substantially increased in the 1990s and the 2000s by purchase, but these acquisitions were mainly in the area of textiles and costume regalia. The acceptance of the Leipold gift will enhance our holdings substantially and well-complement the West African material presently on show in the our exhibition *Hidden Treasures*.

Approval of the acceptance of these ten items and the confirmation of June 21 2018 as the formal hand-over/ presentation date to Iziko Museums of South Africa is hereby requested.

With appreciation,

Signature Removed

Hayden Proud
Curator of Historical Collections of Painting and Sculpture
Iziko Museums of South Africa

6 June 2018

Mr. Max Leipold African Masks Bequest

ID Accession	Classification ID	Item title / Description	Dimension	Item name	Category	Image
2018/102:1	African Art Collection	Ceremonial mask/ (Feminine guardian of the initiation camp/ Ivory Coast)	Dimension: 25cm x 14 cm	Unknown maker	Sculpture	
2018/102:2	African Art Collection	Ceremonial mask after the original (The Baule carved for tourist trade since 1900, as they were renowned as excellent sculptors)	Dimension: 30cm x 14,5 cm	Unknown maker	Sculpture	
2018/102:3	African Art Collection	Ceremonial mask (Fire guardian mask, used to alert community of danger of fire)	Dimension: 24cm x 14 cm	Unknown maker	Sculpture	
2018/102:4	African Art Collection	Ceremonial mask (Feminine mask used in entertainment/possibly Baule)	Dimension: 23cm x 14 cm	Unknown maker	Sculpture	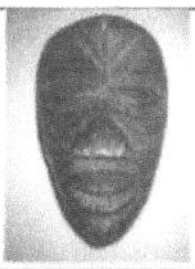
2018/102:5	African Art Collection	Ceremonial mask after the original with Baule features. (The Baule carved for tourist trade since 1900, as they were renowned as excellent sculptors).	Dimension: 42cm x 16 cm	Unknown maker	Sculpture	
2018/102:6	African Art Collection	Ceremonial mask (Bird or beak mask used at ritual events)	Dimension: 34cm x 16 cm	Unknown, maker	Sculpture	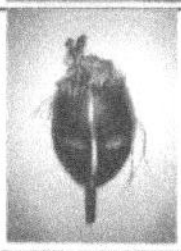

2018/102.7	African Art Collection	Ceremonial mask (Made after the original in the continuing tradition of Ivoirian wood carvers) Mask / Ivory Coast / Dan (Guro) people	Dimension: 44cm x 11 cm	Unknown, maker	Sculpture	
2018/102.8	African Art Collection	Ceremonial mask (Bugle style) (Continues to be used in ceremonial dances) Ivory Coast /Dan people (N'Guere or Bete)	Dimension: 23cm x 15 cm	Unknown, maker	Sculpture	
2018/102.9	African Art Collection	Mask/ Kanyoke Mask (DRC) (Rare only 5 or 6 Known specimens)	Dimension:	Unknown, maker	Sculpture	
2018/102.10	African Art Collection	Unknown (Mask)	Dimension:	Unknown, maker	Sculpture	

www.ingramcontent.com/pod-product-compliance
Lightning Source LLC
LaVergne TN
LVHW041716190726
843493LV00007B/2111